BEATE NOT THE POORE DESK

A Writer to Young Writers

Published by

RABBIT ROOM PRESS

3321 Stephens Hill Lane

Nashville, Tennessee 37013

info@rabbitroom.com

Cover design by Chris Tobias

Cover illustration © 2016 by Jamin Still

Edited by Pete Peterson

ISBN 978-0-9863818-7-4

First Edition

Printed in the United States of America

16 17 18 19 — 6 5 4 3 2 1

BEATE NOT
THE POORE DESK

A Writer to Young Writers

WALTER WANGERIN, JR.

RABBIT ROOM
— PRESS —

This book is dedicated to the Rabbit Room.

Whoso shall tell a tale after a man,
He must rehearse as nigh as ever he can
Every which a word, if it be in his charge,
All speak his rubric be it never so large,
Or else he must repeat his tale untrue,
Feigning the thing, or finding words anew.
                                        —*Geoffrey Chaucer*

1. First Questions

I F YOU SAY TO ME, "I want to be a writer," I will ask, "Why?"

If you answer, "Because I have something to say," or "I've got a novel in me (a play, a screenplay) just waiting to come out." Or if you say, "I like to write poetry about my feelings." Or, "I like to watch strangers and imagine what their lives are like," I will say, "Friend, do something else."

But if you say, "I enjoy words, sentences." Or, "I want to write like Graham Green, Joyce Carol Oates, George Herbert . . ." If you say, "I love writing for its own sake," I will answer, "And the craft?"

"The craft?" you'll say. "Yes. I am hungry to learn the craft."

"Then go for it," I'll say, "and I will teach you. Write first. Practice the craft. Work at developing your skills. Talk to writers or find a good teacher. Discuss your projects with insightful readers. Revise, revise, and even before you find your own voice, the writing itself will reveal your truths.

"Write first, and your novel will build itself before your eyes. Dialogue with your characters. Ask the novel how you two (the novel and you yourself) should proceed. Write first, and the *writing* will reveal the deep principles by which you have always ordered and interpreted the world."

How can I know what I want to say until I say it?

How can I know what I will write until I write it?

As the oldest brother of my siblings—myself no older than five years—I used to invent the stories that put my brothers and sisters to sleep. Even after they'd conked out, I would keep telling the story to myself till it was finished, because I wanted to know how it ended.

That sort of thing came naturally to me.

During my third grade year some good person donated a score of typewriters to our school. As soon as I learned to type I started writing my stories on paper. They were foolish and juvenile, of course, but I got a kick out of the practice and, at the same time, got better at it.

And still I told my stories out loud. But now I learned to weave reality into my tapestries—an advance I scarcely realized at the time.

One day Kathy Drees stood up in class and described her experience at the funeral of some relative. She said she stood in line to say goodby. Then she was looking at the old man in his casket. He seemed to be sleeping. She put out her hand and touched the back of his hand, and was shocked at how cold, how *cold* it was.

Well. I thought that her story was pretty good. But I could do better.

So I stood up too and told my own story.

I said that once upon a time I had an older sister. I said that my sister was hit by a car . . .

The sister part was made up. But the hit-by-a-car part was true—only I was the one that had been hit. This was the piece of reality I wove into the tale.

My brother and I were crossing a busy avenue in Chicago. He ran out in front of a bus, then suddenly turned and ran back. But I was already on my way after him. He ran back because a car was coming. I didn't see the car (it was purple and very big) until it was on me. I whirled away from it, but it hit me directly on the butt and sent me ten, fifteen feet through the air when, again, I landed on my butt. The poor driver ran to me. He asked how I was. I was stunned, but not all that hurt.

Nevertheless, the man carried me to the car and put me in the back. Three little girls were already sitting there, so I stood up against the door with my head bent at the ceiling. I told the driver how to get to my house. On the way I peed in my pants and was riven with embarrassment. Before we arrived at the house, I saw my brother Paul walking all alone on the sidewalk, crying so mournfully that he looked like a wolf cub with his face to the sky.

Now then, this was the first half of my story. When I told it, I took the place of my brother, and in my place I put my pretend sister—only she had been *killed* by the car.

So that was already better than Kathy's tale. The death of a sister by car was so much more dramatic than an old man's passing away.

Here was the second half, and it was a doozy.

When *I* was at the funeral, and when *I* was at the casket of my poor, pure white sister (I named her Karen), my mother told me to *kiss* her. So I kissed her, and my lips were cold, cold for a week thereafter.

I sat down, proud of my performance—and a far piece more skillful than I had been before.

The upshot was not as happy.

When I got home that afternoon, both my teacher and the school principal were sitting in the living room. So persuasive had my tale been that they believed it. They had come to commiserate with my mother for her loss.

My mother met me not with praise but with punishment. But I thought she didn't understand. I hadn't been telling lies. This is how a good story is told.

A writer has to overcome such jealousy. But that there was jealousy at all signified a fierce affection for his choice of words—that what he had written, he had written.

That summer I wrote my first novel. It was based on Einstein's belief that time was fluid. I imagined that there were two twins, one of whom left the earth to travel through space. When he returns only a year older than when he left, behold, his brother is an old man.

Through college and into my marriage I stayed up late into the night writing stories, writing stories, consciously improving my craft.

When I satisfied myself that I had finally produced a worthy novel, I sent the manuscript to something like thirteen publishers. They all rejected it—except that an editor at Harper & Row rejected the piece with a long letter of explanation. She persuaded me of its unfixable errors. (My jealousy had resolved itself into a hungry practicality.)

I wrote her immediately asking whether she might consider a second novel. She said she might.

In a year I sent her a book I entitled *The Book of the Dun Cow*. In the end Harper & Row accepted it, and I was on my way.

Now, I DON'T OFFER my experience as a model for your own. My intent is to explain the signs of an author's natural abilities and the steps whereby he discovers and develops his craft.

It doesn't matter at what age you make these discoveries. As a creative writing professor I have often read the talents in a student before she knows what she has, and then have introduced her to her writing self. That may be enough to send her on her way.

Again, my experience:

In my senior year of high school I took a creative writing class taught by a Mr. James Barbour. In his youth this man's face had been ravaged by a severe case of acne. The scars, in fact, run up into his hairline. Mr. Barbour often sat in his chair on one buttock only. He said he had a carbuncle on the other. His voice was high and nasal. He smoked cigarettes in class. We admired him.

Mr. Barbour returned our first stories by plopping them down on our desks starting with the front rows and ending with the back. My name begins with *W.* Therefore, I sat in the back. Mine was the last desk, and I the last student to catch my story.

As Mr. Barbour walked back to the front of the classroom, he said, "Wangerin can write the eyes out of a turkey at fifty paces."

At the time I scarcely knew what he meant, but I knew it was a compliment (better yet, a compliment spoken in the language of a professional, as if I were myself already a professional), and straightway I sent the story off to a magazine—which rejected it.

Today I understand James Barbour's judgment of my work. My use of detail was sharp and accurate. As a result I can still repeat that story, in spite of all the years that have passed between.

Take your compliments to heart, even though you may have to feed on them until you are (as I was) thirty years old. Long years of famine should not altogether discourage you.

I. Art: Its Dynamics and Its Potency

2. A Working Definition

ART IS AN ACT, A process. In order to be complete, writing requires a reader.

Art occurs. It happens. It is always an *event* rather than an object. It is a verb, not a noun, though it is by means of nouns that art takes place.

Art is its own peculiar form of human communication.

As such, the complete event is divided into two parts: first, the artist acts.

The artist Rembrandt paints a picture of St. Paul in prison.

After long preparation—learning his craft and living his life both consciously and unconsciously, earning thereby a life-long wisdom—he conceives the idea for his subject. The artist enters his studio alone. Perhaps he makes pencil drawings of Paul's figure, his posture, the outlines of his face. This is an act. Rembrandt tightens his canvas on a wooden frame and sets it on an easel. He selects and mixes brown, tenebrous colors, dabs his brush, and begins to paint. Where he chooses to touch the brush to the canvas will not be where the viewer's eyes first will fall, because these choices belong to two separate people and two separate acts.

As long as the painting hangs in the dark room of a closed museum, the process is only half finished. Its second half begins when we come in daylight, and look, and enter the world of Rembrandt's imagined prison cell—when *we* begin to act.

In a kind of spiritual motion, step by step, we peer deeper into the painting. We may start with the apostle's body entire. He sits in a disheveled robe, the source of the light outside the frame. Next we may follow his finger, which points to the book on his lap, though Paul's eyes are up. He is not reading. But *we* do, and so discover that the book is a Bible, and his finger is on a particular passage in the Bible. Then our sight may ascend to the stark, red-rimmed eyes. This is an act on our part. It becomes an emotional act when we shudder at how haunted are his eyes: Paul is an apostle smitten by theology!

So, then: two distinct acts make a whole.

Only by the viewer's responding act does the artist move outside himself into a community, into communion with society—or else his work must exist within his experience alone. Only by releasing his art does he acknowledge the "other" who will also shape the thing as it grows before him and within him. First, the artist composes in sensible detail. Second, we participate in his composition when we respond to its details—details able to be sensed, imagined, felt, *experienced*.

Altogether, then, I define the full double-act of art as Composed Experience.

Even though the artists of a single piece may number in the hundreds, generations following generations in the long labor; and even though the viewers can number in the millions over several millenia; and even though the thing created is enormous, intricate, and profoundly complex, nevertheless, art remains an act completed in two parts.

The pyramids are obvious examples.

But I have another work in mind, which I have experienced myself: The cathedral in Chartres, built in the thirteenth century.

I saw its two dissimilar steeples across the surrounding plain. They struck me with their majesty and moved me by their heavenward reach.

It was a wondrous façade.

When I entered its doors and then its great nave, the architecture would not let me stand still. The columns called me forward, for they stood in rhythmic rows of two different kinds, one sort of column following the next like rhymes in a poem. They seemed impossibly slender, raising my eyes and lifting my soul to the vaults and the traceries of the cosmos.

I know now that their delicate slenderness was accomplished by an optical illusion: each column thickened the higher it soared, making the whole seem straight and marvelously tall.

Forward, I say, toward the high, canopied altar, which was the glory of God.

And the whole nave—its statuary, its polished floor, its side chapels—was washed in a soft cerulean blue, causing the stones themselves to seem velvet. I've never known such a blue. It shed from the stained glass of the great rose window behind me, glass colored by what was then a new process.

And the organ played.

The cathedral murmured, "Grandeur," to me. And to my soul, "You move in the holy house of God."

My experience within this monumental work of art was a train of powerful emotions. It was a spiritual drama.

But without my response, the art of Chartres Cathedral would remain only half finished. The entire building and all its accoutrements would have remained an object merely, the *potential* of art, but in itself not yet art.

This then—the artist, the work, and the audience together—is the Composed Experience. *Art.*

3. Art Weaves New Worlds

S O: YOU WOULD BE A writer. Know, then, the powerful effect of your work when it is done and done well.

The reader who experiences your story can actually be shaped in her mind, in her perceptions, in her spirit—especially if the reader is a child or someone suffering the confusion of a crisis: the death of her beloved, a divorce, a hysterectomy. Art can order what is otherwise a distressing mess. It can offer worth to those who think themselves worthless, and a name to those who are nameless.

Homer's *Odyssey* revealed to the Greeks what it was to be Greek.

Likewise, another odyssey in the book of Exodus—the Hebrews' escape from slavery and their wandering the wilderness as they traveled to the Promised Land—shaped the knowledge of the children of Israel: they were a peculiar people with a peculiar purpose, a nation chosen by God to be his own.

Still today the tale is told at every Passover celebration.

IN 1980 MY FAMILY and I moved from a suburb in Evansville, Indiana—mostly white—into the inner city, mostly African American.

Our youngest daughter had been adopted. In those days she was called "bi-racial" because her birth-mother was white and her birth-father black. Talitha, therefore, was a light-skinned child ("high-yaller," in an older parlance). She had "good hair" since it was naturally straight. Her features could have been Hispanic or Middle Eastern, though they were also an admixture of African American. Her eyebrows were finely etched, her black lashes long and cupping sunlight, her mouth a perfect cupid's bow. Her head was shaped like a lightbulb, narrowing down to the small ball of her chin.

Among whites Talitha was considered black. Among blacks she was considered white. Neither judgment was always rendered kindly. In what society, then, could the child feel at home? Who *was* she?

One Sunday, Talitha and I were walking along a row of shotgun houses. These buildings had been constructed quickly during the Second World War, but had not been torn down when the war ended. Now, more than forty years later, they were a most inexpensive habitation. Some were clean and very well kept. Others were dilapidated and home to the poor.

As we walked we heard an angry shout from a house ahead of us. I thought it was a man's shout. But then the screen door was whacked open, and a boy about Talitha's age flew out backward—had been *thrown* out—and landed on his bum.

An enraged woman stepped out and pointed at him. A woman. Not a man. I took her to be the boy's mother.

"Do me a favor," she yelled at the boy. "Do me a favor and die!"

She slammed back into the house.

Talitha made a moan of pity.

She released my hand and went to the boy, who was still sitting on the sidewalk, on his bum, with an empty face.

She said something like, "Are you okay?"

Immediately the boy jumped up and pointed his finger at Talitha and yelled, "Do me a favor! Do me a favor and die!"

When I came and took her hand, she said miserably, "Tell me my story."

It was my habit in those days to invent stories for each of my children. I meant to make them laugh, to enthrall them with a mystery, to comfort them.

Talitha's was a creation story.

That night in her bedroom, I told her the story again.

Here is it in brief.

"Once upon a time," I said, "there was no sky. Do you know what it means," I asked my daughter, "for there to be no sky?"

In the regular liturgy of this event, she answered as she always answered, "No."

So I began to weave a good world around her, in which she was loved and given a bright identity.

"It's like a nightmare where bad things fly out of the blackness, coming to get you. No roof on a house, no blue lid to cover everything.

"But," I said, "God said, 'I am going to make a child. I am going to love her with all my heart. Nothing should ever hurt or scare my beautiful girl.'"

Then I walked through the days of creation.

God climbs to the highest of high and shouts like thunder, "Let there be a hard, firm roof between the evil above and all the space below."

But all the earth below is water, only water. So God stomps the water back to its shores and borders.

God causes food to grow so that his hungry child should eat.

God makes birds and fish and animals with eyes, so that his girl can have talk and company.

As they are created, the animals say, "God, where is it?"

God says, "Where is what?"

And all the animals say, "Where is the child? Where is the little child to lead us? You have to make a child, or who will tell us what our names are?"

"Well, well," says God, "then it's time to make a child."

God strolls the banks of a river, looking for the very best clay. He kneels down and pats the clay into two wonderful lumps, a big one and a smaller one on top. He divides the lower portion of the big lump into two legs. He pops two arms from its sides. Then, with the tips of his fingers on the topmost, smaller lump, God begins to carve a face: two eyes closed, their black lashes shining. Two ears scrolled like seashells. Two eyebrows as clean as raven's wings.

But no air in her lungs. No breath in her nose.

The animals say, "That's the child? It's a statue as cold as stone."

In a little moment the animals are amazed. God is crying. Tears are dropping from his eyes onto the face of the clay-child, and God is washing her with his hands, so that there are two faces glistening now, one above and one below.

And then what? Then the mighty Creator bends down and down, until his lips touch the lips of his girl.

"Do you remember, Talitha? Surely you remember what happened next."

God kisses you.

And while he is kissing you, he breathes out—

which is your first breath in, and your lungs blow up like twin balloons, and your heart goes *Thump!* and starts to beat. The blood flows through you warm and soft and strong.

"Remember? Oh, you ought to remember this, because then you sneezed into the face of God!"

God rocks back. You think he is thundering. But he isn't. He is laughing.

And all the animals are giggling, roaring, bellowing, laughing.

"Then God pokes you in your mouth. He says, 'Girl, I put a tongue in there. Use it. Talk the live-long day.'

"And the live-long day you gossip and chatter."

God pokes you in your arms and legs. "I put motion in there and speed and strength. Run like the wind. Work like the pistons of a locomotive."

Finally, God pokes you in your chest. "I put a heart in there. Love me. Love all the animals. Love your family, my child, exactly as I will always love you."

The child lives the story. She experiences it, and it is true. When she walks outside, she sees the sky as a protection, made personally for her, the girl who must be important since she came from God's love.

She knows wherefrom comes the food she eats. And all the animals of the world, and even her own self. From God.

Where is her home? In the midst of creation.

Who is she? A child of God.

I didn't have to guess whether the story truly formed Talitha's conception of herself. I saw it in action.

Once while the Wangerins were eating lunch in an all-white Hays, Kansas, restaurant, the waitress stepped to our table to take our order.

But before she asked her first question, she stopped and stared at us as if we were a conundrum: two adults, two children African American, and two children white like their parents.

Suddenly she snapped her fingers. A solution had occurred to her. She smiled and said, "Field trip?"

No, no, I said.

New problem. And a new solution:

"These are your children, right?"

Yes, yes.

"So, you adopted."

Yes.

"And," said the waitress slyly, "I know which ones you adopted." She pointed her pencil at black Matthew. "That one," she said, "and," pointing at Talitha, "that one."

Yes. What a fine mind, and what keen observation you have.

Having satisfied herself that the world had been put to rights again, the waitress took our order and walked toward the kitchen door.

Talitha whispered to me, "I know how that lady knows I'm adopted."

How, child?

My daughter stood up on her chair and threw out her arms and cried, "Because I'm *black*!"

The waitress hesitated a beat before pushing through the door.

IN 1774 WOLFGANG VON GOETHE published *Die Leiden des jungen Werthers*, an epistolary novel whose English title is *The Sorrows of Young Werther*.

Think of this work as the slim waist of an hour glass.

The sands that flow down into the novel (the glass's waist) are Goethe's experiences, gathered adroitly by means of his craft. The sands that collect in the bottom are the experiences of the novel's readers. Goethe shaped the first. Then, in his time, the novel shaped the lives of many a hyper-romanticized young man.

We can identify three distinct events which filled and impelled Goethe's story.

When he was an emotional twenty-three years old, Goethe became infatuated with a young woman named Charlotte Buff. But Charlotte was the fiancée of his friend G. C. Kestner. To love a woman already betrothed and impossible to gain caused great, mute suffering. But then to have to give her up and leave her—well, that was anguish.

Hold that thought.

The next experience was not his own. But it gave him an alternative ending *to* his own. A tragic ending. A certain Karl Wilhelm Jerusalem, the secretary of the Brunswick ambassador, suffered the snubs of the aristocratic dandies of the court. Then Jerusalem's superior reprimanded him in public. Finally, like Goethe, he fell in love with the wife of a colleague whom he could not have. With a flick of her tongue she dismissed him. And so in October 1772 the poor man committed suicide.

Goethe's third experience occurred when he was at dinner in the house of a self-confident burgher named Brentano, the husband of Maximiliane, for whom Goethe held tender feelings.

Perhaps unconscious of the brutality of its effect, the jealous Brentano uttered some remark which tore at Goethe's tender heart. Crushed, Geothe left his dinner unfinished.

However insignificant this event might seem, it fused his two previous experiences and crystallized the shape of his novel.

Young Werther loves, agonizes, is emotionally cudgeled, and finally kills himself.

Now, then, to the readers.

During the latter part of the eighteenth century, young Europeans were reacting against the facile optimism of the previous generation ("God's in his heaven. All's right with the world."). They hated its cool rationalism, its scorn for matters of the heart. The new generation sought a world that revolved around the individual, a world in which blooming nature overgrew the bones of a pure sterile intellect.

This was a period in Europe of *Sturm und Drang*, "Storm and Stress," of *weltschmerz*, "world weariness and pain." Passion became a life-principle, whether in joy or in *leiden*, "sorrows."

Goethe's novel gave name and a shape to these feelings, feelings that became so intense they became known as *Wertherfieber*, "Werther fever."

And this was the force of his art. Once it was published, Europeans were so persuaded by its "truth" (as they reckoned the truth) that an astonishing number of young men did themselves in. Like Werther, they commited suicide.

For the sake of identity, of self-worth, and for freedom, for safety, or for danger, art can weave new worlds. And those who enter and inhabit them are genuinely changed thereby.

4. The Peculiar Experience

ARTISTIC LITERARY COMPOSITION HAS THE potential to engage its reader in an experience distinct from most other sorts of human experience. Its effect is in its form.

Along with trauma and other experiences of high intensity—dramatic reversals, wonderful successes, egregious sins, natural and social and personal disasters, loss of virginity, marriage, the births of children, crime, courtrooms, divorce, the crashings of income and support, death, and the like—an experience composed by a crack artist may have the power to seize a soul and hold it; may alter the perceptions of an individual, his beliefs, and sometimes his behaviors; may work changes that can linger long, and longer still if the artful experience repeats itself in, say, ritual and if the individual is willing.

I list below the characteristics by which the artistic experience has the unique power to transfigure a reader.

IT IS *DISCRETE*. I mean that it has a clear, sharp beginning and a recognizable ending—and within these two the whole tale exists. "Once upon a time" promises a "they lived happily ever after." It is the same whether or not these formulae are used, whether or not the end ends happily. "Tick" will have its "tock."

All other experiences come without starts. They issue from previous experiences and bleed into the next.

So let's say you get up in the morning and eat breakfast and dress and go to work and work and lunch and work and drive home again. It's all a blur of sequels. On the other hand, let's say that going home you have a car accident. And the other driver is at fault. And you are angry. Though these still appear in a wash of experiences, when you do finally get home and tell someone what happened to you, *now* you will make a story of it. Now it is lifted from the muddy rest of your day, for now you give it a sort of beginning ("Let me tell you what happened to me!") and at some point you will come to an ending ("What do you think of *that*?")

It's very likely that this discretely separated event will cause your listener to imagine the accident for herself. She will see, feel, and participate in what you saw, felt, and experienced. She will *be* at the accident just as you were. She'll receive it from your point of view. If she is truly involved, she'll not only sense your anger, but became angry too.

You may have told the tale artlessly. You may have included unnecessary details or left out necessary ones; you may have used words that blur the story. No matter. By the simple process of distinguishing this experience from others, you've succeeded in turning an event into a story.

In January 1909 when he was about forty years old, the French author Marcel Proust drank a cup of tea and munched on a rusk biscuit. Immediately the taste of these reminded him of a similar experience he'd had as a child. By his present response that experience was separated and elevated above others, and with that memory there rushed into his mind a whole train of experiences that had remained unconscious, such as the landscape and the people of his boyhood holidays.

All at once Proust had the beginning and the material for a long autobiographical novel he entitled *The Remembrance of Things Past*. With *Remembrance*, so powerfully and so finely written, he entered the pantheon of great writers.

THE SECOND CHARACTERISTIC WHICH gives a composition its unique effect on a reader is that the work has an *internal integrity*.

I mean that it is written without one extraneous detail, nor does it lack a single significant detail. It has been smoothed like a stone in a stream. It is like a fairy tale told by generations of mothers and grand-mothers until the thing has been reduced to its basic element. Everything, *everything*, works together to weave a tapestry clean and whole. All of its parts, its images, descriptions, sensations, actions are united so that a reader's experience is made most persuasive and powerful.

The force of many details thus harmonized may catch the whole of a childlike reader and enliven her as with the rhythmic beating of her heart.

Read—*listen* to—the following poem by Robert Frost. Its title is "Bereft." Its mood is melancholy. The rhymed repetition of the long *o*'s and the four-beat rhythm of each line draws us deeper and deeper into the poet's experience. Likewise, the building of its imagery (from the sound of the wind to a door before a seashore, and the weather, and times, and the season; to the porch and to leaves on the porch; to the loneliness of the house; to the spiritual loneliness of the narrator) and the back-and-forth of its setting (from where the narrator stands to the wide outside) walk us all the way to God.

> *Where had I heard this wind before*
> *Change like this to a deeper roar?*
> *What would it take my standing there for,*

Holding open a restive door,
Looking down hill to a frothy shore?
Summer was past and day was past.
Somber clouds in the west were massed.
Out in the porch's sagging floor,
Leaves got up in a coil and hissed,
Blindly struck at my knee and missed.
Something sinister in the tone
Told me my secret must be known:
Word I was in the house alone
Somehow must have gotten abroad,
Word I was in my life alone,
Word I had no one left but God.

"Word, word, word," for the poem itself is constructed of words, of their meanings and their dark sounds.

One more example, one of the tightest, most potent works I know: the anonymous, Scottish "Edward, Edward."

It is both a poem—a ballad—and a short story. And because the whole comes in a dialogue between a mother and her son, the poet never allows himself to show, nor does he tell us, how we ought to feel: "Just the facts, ma'am."

I will modernize the poem by changing the spellings and translating dated words into contemporary words, though the sounds of the old are always more thrilling than the new. The first verse of the old:

> *"Why dois your brand sae drap wi bluid,*
>   *Edward, Edward?*
> *Why dois your brand sae drap wi bluid,*
>   *And why sae sad gang yee O?"*
> *"O I hae killed my hauké sae guid,*
>   *Mither, mither.*
> *O I hae killed my hauké sae guid,*
>   *And I had nae mair bot hee O."*

And here it is with my changes:

> *"Why does your sword so drop with blood,*
>   *Edward, Edward?*
> *Why does your sword so drop with blood,*
>   *And why so sadly go you O?"*
> *"O I have killed my hawk so good,*
>   *Mother, mother,*
> *O I have killed my hawk so good.*
>   *And I had no more but he O."*

> *"Your hawk's blood was never so red,*
>   *Edward, Edward,*
> *Your hawk's blood was never so red,*
>   *My dear son I tell you O."*
> *"O I have killed my red-roan steed,*
>   *Mother, mother,*
> *O I have killed my red-roan steed*
>   *That once was so fair and free O."*

"*Your steed was old, and you have more,*
  Edward, Edward,
Your steed was old, and you have more,
  Some other grief do you grieve O."
"*O I have killed my father dear,*
  Mother, mother,
O I have killed my father dear,
  Alas and woe is me O!"

"*And what penance will you suffer for that,*
  Edward, Edward?
And what penance will you suffer for that,
  My dear son, now tell me O."
"*I'll set my feet in yonder boat,*
  Mother, mother,
I'll set my feet in yonder boat,
  And I'll fare over the sea O."

"*And what will you do with your towers and your hall,*
  Edward, Edward?
And what will you do with your towers and your hall,
  That were so fair to see O?"
"*I'll let them stand till they down fall,*
  Mother, mother,
I'll let them stand till they down fall,
  For here never more must I be O."
"*And what will you leave to your children and wife,*
  Edward, Edward?

And what will you leave to your children and wife
    When you go over the sea O?"
"The whole world's room. Let them beg through life,
    Mother, mother,
The whole world's room. Let them beg through life,
    For them never more will I see O."

"And what will you leave to your own mother dear,
    Edward, Edward?
And what will you leave to your own mother dear,
    My dear son, now tell me O."
"The curse of hell from me shall you bear,
    Mother, mother,
The curse of hell from me shall you bear,
    Such counsels you gave to me O."

Boom!

In the last lines the whole is revealed, and we must
go back to the beginning and read the poem in a new
and tragic light. His *mother* sent him to kill his father,
and all the rest, step by step, is lost. She already knows
the cause of the blood. Edward prevaricates twice, twice
forcing her to play the lie. In those days a falcon and its
master were in an intimate communion, so this is like
the loss of his father. But falconry was a sometime thing.
To kill his horse was to kill transport and strength and
sincere companionship. But he killed neither falcon nor
horse, and we are shocked with the truth.

But *we* are taken aback. The violence never disorders or troubles the objectivity of the poem. Our horror contrasts with the poem's decorum, which intensifies the wallop at the end. And the cool repetition of "Edward, Edward" and "Mother, mother" mounts to the clash between the two.

Now then, can you find a single passage, a single word, that should be cut without ruining the ballad's effect? Or can you think of anything the ballad left out?

This is what I mean by *internal integrity*.

WHEN THE SECOND CHARACTERISTIC of the artistic experience works well, the third is already in place.

It is the involvement of the whole of the reader: her calculating mind, all her senses (in the cauldron of her imagination), her affective heart and emotions, her moral judgments, the sensations in her body, laughter, fearful anticipations. The piece, while it is being read, becomes *the reader's universe*. For the moment she dwells nowhere else but in the story.

You go to the theater. You sit. The room darkens. The screen brightens. If the movie is a good one, your critical mind shuts down, and you enter the movie completely.

This is what is called the willing suspension of disbelief.

No longer are you aware of your "real" place. The movie has become your place and all places. No longer do you think about chronological time. The second hand of your wristwatch has stopped. The watch itself has vanished. The movie is a sort of *kairos* time. As it unfolds, the story contains all time. Creation begins after the opening credits, and creation comes to its ending when the legend appears and says, "The End."

Then, walk out of the theater. Sunlight astonishes you. The "real" world surprises you, because the movie-world was your universe till then. But when you walk out, you are not quite the person that you were. Your experience has in some slight way re-shaped you.

Let's stick with movies a little while longer. They can have a cumulative effect.

Consider how many pit good guys against the bad. Cowboys are good. So are sheriffs, spies, armies, detectives, the FBI, those who "walk tall" (and carry big sticks), innocent folk, doctors, lawyers, and on and on—all against some malicious enemy. With whom do you think the audience identifies? Of course: *we* are the good guys. And once the badness of the bad guys is established, why, we have every right to use fair means and foul to defeat them. They fight? We fight better. They break rules? So do we—but all in a good cause, which justifies our own lawlessness.

On the one hand, such stories comfort the prejudices and the proclivities we bring to them. We go to the movies already convinced of our goodness. The movie verifies our convictions.

Scripture misconstrued can also justify bad behavior. Noah has three sons: Shem, Ham, and Japheth. Ham is the father of Canaan. It is Ham who commits the offense of walking into his father's tent and seeing the old man drunk and naked. When Noah comes out of his hangover, he curses Ham's children with a terrible curse:

Cursed be Canaan, lowest of slaves shall he be to his brothers.

It is by this exact passage that slave holders argued the rightness of keeping African Americans downtrodden as the lowest of slaves, for they were doing nothing more than carrying out a divine command.

On the other hand, children and the innocent among us are shaped by the movie's universe: henceforward they shall divide the world into two parts only. A United States president gets away with naming certain nations evil. Never, never do we go to war except our enemies deserve our righteous might. They are subhuman and brutal. We are the children of God.

Everyone whom we consider the "other" is fodder for our slaughters.

Even so has it been since folk told fairy tales about witches and giants. Since the children of Israel entered the Promised Land. Since legends praised heroes and hated their foes.

There is a vast quantity of literature that calls readers into a more moral universe, such as Homer's *Illiad*, where enemies are neither altogether good nor altogether bad. Among the Greeks (who win the war), Achilles is flawed. Among the Trojans (who lose), Hector is an admirable man. In Tolstoy's *War and Peace*, the author balances the enmities, giving weight to all sides. And the children of Israel, after all, reject their God as surely as do the Baal-worshipping Canaanites.

But such literature changes individuals one by one, who may change others by their teachings and persuasions. The good-guy/bad-guy sort changes nations.

And its changes affect those who are least conscious of what is happening.

In his essay "Religion and Literature," T. S. Eliot writes:

> *The fiction that we read affects our behavior toward our fellow man, affects our patterns of ourselves. When we read of human beings behaving in certain ways, with the approval of the author, who gives his benediction to this behavior by his attitude toward the result of the behavior arranged by himself, we can be influenced towards behaving the same way.*

And, he writes, that when the audience is youthful enough, not yet altogether formed,

> . . . *what happens is a kind of inundation, [an] invasion of the undeveloped personality, the empty (swept and garnished) room, by the stronger personality of the poet.*

Because such literature has so powerful an effect upon our readers, we are bound to observe a certain ethical restraint, so that our writing leads readers to virtue and not to false or iniquitous behaviors.

I will, in chapters 7 and 8, develop these ethical requirements.

5. Shaping

DURING THE RENAISSANCE, POETS DELIGHTED in the Greek sense of the word "poet." Ben Jonson defined the poet as a "maker," a creator not unlike the Primeval Creator of All.

But C. S. Lewis resisted this somewhat haughty definition. He said that anything a fallen human can create out of whole cloth, completely new, would have to be a monster that never did exist in God's universe, because it is a deviation from the harmonious whole.

Personally, I find the ancient Sanskrit meaning of the word "poet" to be closer to the task I am called to do. The Sanskrit cognate is *cinote*. It defines the artist as "a heaper into heaps and a piler into piles."

We artists bring our crafty attentions to the stuff of the world as though it were a mess of pick-up sticks, a helpless chaos. In order to compose the sticks into a smooth-stoned and unifying story, we have to organize them, arrange them, put them into some kind of order. It is our job to heap certain things here and to pile other things over there, until we've made a kind of sense of it all. *That's* what we make. Sense.

Revisit "Edward, Edward." Its sticks are built into the structure of a single powerful experience.

Literature *is* order in chaos. Our songs, stories, poems, screenplays, plays do more than persuade others that order exists: they construct the house in which the reader can dwell, through whose windows the messy world becomes—for good or for ill—a labeled cosmos.

Even existentialists like Albert Camus, who find no meaning at all in this "dense" and cluttered existence, order things by writing novels (*The Stranger, The Plague*).

Perhaps the most telling word by which to define the artist's effect upon his audience is the Old English *scop*. It's pronounced "shop." It is the cognate of our contemporary word "shape." To shape: to shape a people by singing their histories; to shape the grief of their days into a hopefulness for their futures; to shape their dreams into realities.

In his novel *Grendel*, John Gardner gives an account of the influence of the art of a scop. Gardner writes of the blind singer who appears in Hrothgar's famous meadhall that by his song he could bring even the hills "low by language."

*He knew his art. He was the king of the Shapers,
harpstring scratchers (oakmoss-bearded, inspired
by winds). He would sing the glory of Hrothgar's
line and gild his wisdom and stir up his men to
more daring deeds, for a price. He sang of battles
and marriages, of funerals and hangings, of the
whimperings of beaten enemies, of splendid hunts
and harvests.*

And the consequence of this singer's song visible?
The dream is made real:

*The old man sang of a glorious meadhall whose
light would shine to the ends of the ragged world.
The thought took seed in Hrothgar's mind. It grew.
Hrothgar would build a magnificent meadhall
high on a hill. The things he said seemed true....*

And then *came* true. Laborers of every kind gathered. "For weeks their uproar filled the days and nights." Then, writes Gardner, "the word went out to the races of men that Hrothgar's hall was finished."

The narrator, Grendel himself, though he is in anguish, perceives the effect of the singer's art:

*"Well, he's changed them," I said, and stumbled
and fell on the root of a tree. "Why not?"*

And again:

*"He reshapes the world," I whispered, bellig-
erent. "So his name ["Schop"] implies. He stares
strange-eyed at the mindless world and turns dry
sticks to gold."*

And again:

*His fingers picked infallibly, as if moved by some-
thing beyond his power, and the words stitched
together out of ancient songs, the scenes inter-
woven out of dreary tales, made a vision without
seams, an image of himself yet not-himself: the
projected possibility.*

Composed Experience. Art.

Or let me illustrate this by imagining what must
have happened over and over in those ancient times.

THE LORD OF ONE meadhall challenges another to fight.

At dawn one morning the comitatuses of each Lord
take sides across a grassy valley. Neither immediately
attacks the other. Instead they hurl violent insults at one
another, taunts meant to swell themselves and to break
the spirits of the enemy. This lasts several hours, till the
sun is fully up and neither army has backed down.

Then the men run at each other and begin the job of hacking. Their armor, their helmets, their shields are of thick leather. Their swords are short, nothing like the long Excalibur King Arthur wielded. Men must come face to face in order to engage each other, cursing and cutting, fighting and foining. Blood makes the grass slick. Many slip and fall without a whack, get up, and go at it again. Women stand on the sidelines making ululations of encouragement.

Few men actually die, though many are maimed and others lie bleeding.

Before the night, when demons will roam abroad to steal the soul of any man left alive, the armies leave off fighting. They gather their wounded and their dead.

Let's say that one of our warriors is dead. Ecglaf the Intrepid. We carry him up to our meadhall on the hill and lay him out in the long building. We kindle the fire that runs the hall from the door to the Lord's dais. Our lord sits down in his carved chair and hangs his head. We eat in misery. We drink mead in misery. Then we stretch ourselves sleepless.

The Shaper takes his lyre and begins to sing. His song, too, is sung in misery, putting words and music to our mourning.

"Yes, yes," we say. "Yes, Ecglaf is dead." The Shaper sings of blood and sorrow. He sings the iron facts of the day.

But then, without a break, the Shaper changes his

song. Now there is no blood. There is glory in the death
of Ecglaf.

And we mumur, "Yes, this is true too."

Soon the Shaper is singing a song familiar to us. It
is a song of the comfort of the Lord God. We sing it
when God is near and when our souls are wrapped in
his numinous presence, when faith turns to devotion
and assurance.

But the Shaper is giving the old song new words.
He names Ecglaf. Ecglaf is being borne to heaven with
victory and honor. We are nodding, "Yes, yes." His
music persuades us of the heroism of our brother. We
leave grief behind. The fire grows warmer. The song
sings thanks to God, and we are, every one of us,
grateful.

We drink mead again, but this time in triumph.

And the day itself is changed.

Now then: when in the future we remember this
battle and the glory of Ecglaf, which day will we say is
true? The day of the horrors of a failing war? Not at all.
We will tell a tale of everlasting nobility. That day will
have taken the place of the other.

It is in this way that art establishes order in chaos
and builds a house of safety after all—and all our
histories ever thereafter will not be the same as if the
Shaper had never shaped that day at all.

6. Naming

O F GOETHE'S NOVEL *The Sorrows of Young Werther* (see Chapter 3, "Art Weaves New Worlds"), Thomas Carlyle writes that the book gave expression to

The nameless unrest and longing discontent which was then agitating every bosom.

Which is to say, Goethe gave a habitation and a name to otherwise undefined, inchoate stirrings in romantic breasts.

HOW OFTEN HAS A reader laid down her book and said, "I always knew this (some vague idea, some mood or internal experience, some quality of love, or her indecipherable response to an event), but I never knew it like *this* before"?

In such cases, art has given a name to that for which

she had no name. More than that, the artistic piece has *become* that name, and now she more than understands it personally, she can talk about it to others. It has entered her conversation.

Here is how the Hebrews told the tale:

In the beginning God created the universe by speaking it into existence. This is the primal language which none but the Creator can speak.

But then he spoke in another sort of language: he named what he had created.

When God cried, "Light!" light burst forth. Indeed, the word "light" was light itself, as if he had opened his mouth and light breathed out.

That light and its temporal period he called "day."

Its dimming and the period of its absence he called "night."

Having uttered the firmament into place, he named it "sky."

The gathered waters became "seas."

And the dry land, "earth."

Then God gave this second naming-language to the man he had created, and the man too spoke it.

> *Out of the ground the Lord God formed every animal of the field and every bird of the air, and brought them to the man to see what he would call them; and whatever the man called every living creature, that was its name.*

Moreover, the man named the woman, which was as much as naming human relationship. He said,

"This at last is bone of my bones and flesh of my flesh. She shall be called 'Woman,' for out of Man was she taken."

What God gave to Adam has been passed down through the ages to the artist.

It is crucial to understand that this biblical naming did more than simply associate a particular sound with a particular thing, as we might say "door," pointing at its object, a bathroom door. For the Hebrews, language was an action. It finished the creation, as it were, of the thing named, and did so in three distinct ways.

1. The thing which is, but is not named, cannot be known. If you have no word for it, you can't talk about it or think on it or consider it or meditate upon it. It may, by God's command, exist. But it exists only in its potential.

To name a thing (as art does) is to clothe it in visibility. To name a thing is to make it knowable, to grant it its place in the human conception of the world; therefore it seems suddenly to appear—graspable.

2. That which has been given a word-name is thereby joined to the whole grammar of all things

named. As words are fashioned into a sentence, so this word now stands in a living relationship with every word in the sentence. And sentences, when they are strung together, encompass all knowledge. As one word may enjoy an infinite variety of grammatical relationships, sentence to sentence, speech to speech, as the *changings* of relationship indicate the healthy flow of its life, even so may the thing named (or the person named) enjoy the development of the countless cross-relationships in the grand creation of God.

3. Finally, the name of a thing can also contain the purpose and the value of that thing. It offers continually a *why*, a reason for that thing's participation in the fullness of creation.

A biblical illustration:

Jacob's name defines his character. He is Ja-akob, a "trickster," a "usurper," for he by cunning tricked his twin brother, Esau, out of his birthright. Next, when their father had grown old and wanted to bless his eldest son, Jacob usurped Esau's blessing by pretending to *be* Esau. In a rage Esau sought to kill Jacob. So Jacob high-tailed it eastward to hide with uncle Laban. Laban, too, was a cunning man. He tricked Jacob to work not seven but fourteen years in order to win the hand of the beautiful Rachel. In return Jacob tricked Laban and amassed large flocks of sheep before he sneaked back to his father's land.

At the dried brook called the Jabbok, Jacob sends his household and all his possessions across while he remains behind. In the night "a man wrestled with him until daybreak."

The "man" says to Jacob, "What is your name?"

Jacob answers, "Jacob."

The "man" says, "You shall no longer be called Jacob, but Israel, for you have striven with God and with man, and have prevailed."

The "man" is God. It is with God that Jacob has been wrestling his whole life long.

But now an Israel is not a Jacob. It means "one who strives with God": a pun, since he who strove with God will hereafter strive on God's side. The name changes Jacob. Arrogance is abolished. Instead, when he approaches Esau, he bows in genuine humility, bows seven times to the ground until he comes near his brother.

The name "Israel" contains the purpose of the descendants of Jacob, the children of Israel, for they become a kingdom of priests. It is Israel who stands between the nations and the Lord, serving the nations by enacting the will of God before them, serving God by bringing (as Moses did) the prayers of the people to him.

It is precisely this sort of naming that art *is* and that art accomplishes.

Most children do at some time suffer panics of abandonment. It can feel like an internal lurch of homesickness, but is otherwise amorphous and greater than the child. Likewise, adults grieving a death fairly drown under their overwhelming, most grievous abandonment. The folktale "Hansel and Gretel" names that feeling and gives it form by storying it.

Hansel and Gretel, brother and sister, are led away from home by their parents into the tangled and pathless world, and there are left to fend from themselves, the two of them alone. But Hansel has prepared a path—not into the future, but back to their house. His scheme doesn't work. For the second time they are led away. This time Hansel drops breadcrumbs, and two things happen. He throws behind them their food and all their sustenance. (Home, you see, was the place of food, and food is love.) And second, harsh nature (birds) destroys the path. Now they are truly abandoned, and the child who hears the tale can consciously grasp and understand the shape and substance of a feeling otherwise foggy in her mind.

But the story does more than that. It walks them through their sad situation to a fine solution, which is also named—and behold: the solution is in themselves.

They come to the hovel of a witch, who represents the cruelty of the wide world. The witch takes them in and feeds them, but this food is only a seeming solution, for soon the witch throws Hansel into a stable and locks him behind a grated door.

She says to Gretel, "Cook something good for your brother and make him fat." For she has said to herself, "He will make a dainty mouthful."

Hansel grows fat, all right. But when the dim-eyed witch commands him to poke his finger through the grate that she might test his meatiness, he pokes out a stick instead.

The witch waits four weeks, then goes crazy.

"Gretel!" she cries. "Stir yourself. Bring some water. Let Hansel be fat or thin, tomorrow I will cook him and eat him."

In the morning the witch says, "We will bake him first." So she pushes Gretel to the oven, which is already hot with the flames below it. She says, "Creep in and see if it is properly heated."

But Gretel knows the witch planned to pitch her in and to bake her first and eat both children at once.

So she says, "I don't know how to do it. How do you get in?"

"Silly goose," snaps the witch. "The door is big enough. Just look, I can get in myself." The witch thrusts her head into the oven. Then Gretel drives her far in and slams the iron door and bolts it.

Gretel runs like lightning to her brother and opens his stable and laughs, "Hansel, we are saved. The old witch is dead!"

Name the problem, and name their escape "salvation."

For what she could have known only by the feeling she now knows by the experience. And she, the little child, is herself woven neatly into the fabric of the universe. Her new identity is proof against the devastations of nature and wise against the evil ways of people. And the child has a purpose, which makes her a person of great value: to love and serve and save others, specifically her brother.

WITH THE ARTIST'S POWERS come responsibilities.

Primarily, not to lie. For a little lie can become a national deception. And a cultural falsehood can cause slaughter.

Among Chaucer's *Canterbury Tales* a prioress rises to tell hers. It begins:

> *Ther was in Asye, in a greet citee,*
> *Amonges Cristene folk, a Jewerye,*
> *Sustened by a lord of that contree*
> *For foul usure and lucre of vileynye,*
> *Hateful to Crist and to his compaignye;*
> *And thrugh the strete men myghte ride or wende,*
> *For it was free and open at eyther end.*

At the end of the street was a Christian school for children. Among these children was a widow's son, a most pious child. Whenever he saw the image of Christ's mother, he kneeled and said his *Ave Maria*. Twice daily the child walked that street through Jewery, to school in the morning, home again in the afternoon.

Perhaps we can shift the blame for this tale from the author to his fictive Prioress. Or else shift it to previous generations of Christians who thrilled themselves and enraged their buddies in the telling. But a tale told may be believed. And the tale believed becomes for the faithful the truth.

As he walked, the innocent boy always sang to the Virgin "*O Alma redemptoris.*"

Now, Satan stirred the hearts of the Jews.

From thenceforth the Jews conspired
This innocent out of this world to chase.

They hired a murderer who snatched the sweet small boy and dragged him into an alley.

This cursed Jew hym hente, and heeld hym faste,
And kitte his throte and in a pit hym caste.

The poor widow waited day and night, but her little child did not come home. She sought him everywhere. She asked the Jews if they had seen him.

"She gooth," says the Prioress, "as she were half out of hir mynde."

But the great God interceded.

That child, that gem of chastity, that emerald of martyrdom of ruby bright!—though his throat had been carved open, sat upright and began to sing *Alma redemptoris* so loud that all the place began to ring.

Soon after the child is found, his murderer hears his sentence: "Evil shall have what evil will deserve."

With torment and with shameful deeth echon
This provost dooth thise Jewes for to sterve
That of this mordre wiste, and that anon.
He nolde no swich cursednesse observe,
"Yvele shal have that yvele wol deserve."
Therfore with wilde hors he dide him drawe,
And after that he heng hem by the lawe.

"By the law" of the land of the Christians.

It is not unlike the stories the Romans told of the early Christians, that they killed young babies and ate their flesh and drank their blood.

And on and on.

Bigotries need their names. Stories provide those names.

Only recently has the tale of the fall of man ceased to heap the burning coals of judgment upon all women for dragging men into sin. Until now it has, among the folk, named Eve a traitor to be kept under the virtuous thumbs of the more righteous and longsuffering

Adams. Children—both male and female—heard
the tale, were already in their innocence shaped by
its shape, and did not question the truth of the tale,
though the tale itself (and therefore the culture around
them) had caused their lie to become their truth.

7. Ethical Obligations: 1

T HE POWER OF GOVERNANCE OUGHT not to be used lightly, nor iniquitously.

King Louis IX of France is remembered as Saint Louis. Power in his hands was the benediction of his people. He was a splendid knight whose kindness and engaging manner made him popular. He was a just king. Although he exacted what was due him, he had no wish to wrong anyone, from the lowest peasant to the richest vassal. He often administered justice personally. Memorably, at his Vincennes manor he assembled his subjects at the foot of an oak. He was a pious king. He loved the church. Under his reign he brought peace, and that mostly by diplomacy. Were he a writer of as much dignity, Louis might have been a Charles Dickens or an Oliver Goldsmith.

Henry VII of England was another sort of king altogether. Those who disagreed with him perished.

Given the powerful effect that art (writing) can

have upon its readers, neither should the governance of the mind be used lightly.

Therefore it is my opinion that artists must be conscientious in the use of their craft, acknowledging and adhering to certain ethical standards.

Not rules! Not commandments, for these suggest absolutes. Ethical standards change. They evolve. By "adherence" I mean a living relationship between the author and the shifting standards. And by "relationship" I mean a *covenantal* relationship which wants a common agreement: "Give me your wise counsel," says the reader, "and I will give you my attentions."

IN MY EIGHTH GRADE year at Highland Junior High in Edmonton, Canada, I submitted a story to a school contest.

The story had not been written as a school assignment. By then I was regularly composing on a small German portable typewriter.

The story won first prize—which was to stand on stage and experience the thrill of reading (performing) my work before the entire school assembly.

Now, I had woven the story of fact (the warp) and fiction (the woof). Without considering the righteousness of the matter or the privacy of its principle characters, I'd spun the warp from several problematic events in my family. The fictional woof gave them a most dramatic setting. It collapsed the events into one, multiplying the dramatic force by a factor of three.

So I put my mouth to the standing microphone and delivered the story like Charlton Heston in *The Ten Commandments*, which I'd seen at the age of twelve.

After the assembly filed out, while walking down the hall to history class, I noticed that my classmates and my teachers began to see me in a new light: they honored my perseverance under awful circumstances. At the same time they expressed their sympathy for me.

I sat in the history class right proud of myself. Oh, what a wonderful trick I had played on everyone! Not only did they like my story—they believed it! And because people act on what they believe, belief engenders a new truth. Therefore, while sitting behind the bald head of my teacher, I realized that I was a creator—almost a godly creator—for I had changed the real world just a smidgen, and the change would stick because no one knew what I had accomplished. I was a *secret* creator. But I had lied. Though I was too young to recognize it, I'd broken faith with my audience. I had used my power unethically.

And here was the sign of a committed writer: my father read the story. When he handed it back to me, I saw that he had in his own handwriting revised one phrase. He deleted the phrase "I took out my handy gun." Today, of course, I realize that it was a silly cliché. But at the time I was upset that he had the gall

to change *anything* without first asking me. My words
were my own!

During the second year of my marriage to Ruth-
anne Bohlmann, I spent nights from nine o'clock into
the early hours of the morning, writing—actually, still
practicing at writing—short stories. Thanne went to
bed at nine. The time thereafter was mine.

One night I wrote a story I believed to be the best
I'd ever written. It was tight, concise, and crackling
with imagery. It consisted of two characters only, a
weeny of a husband and a scold of a wife. The wife
dies. The husband enacts revenge upon her corpse.

In the morning I took the story to Thanne and
asked what she thought of it.

She said, "This is a bad story."

"No," I said, and began to point out the integrated
plot, the abbreviated, hectic sentences while the husband was taking his wife's criticisms. The language
"snapped," as I told her, "like tiny firecrackers."

"Hey," I said. "It's a *good* story."

She said, "I'm not talking about the writing. I'm
talking about the morality."

When I sat down to revise it, my rereading of the
manuscript put me to shame. I had exchanged decency
for smut. To get it "right" does not always mean to make it
"righteous." Thanne's observation had two consequences:

Once again I was taught the power of literature, to
change minds, to shape attitudes, to shift the world,

if ever so slightly. It damages the world to be shifted with a lie and with cruelty for cruelty's sake. There had to be an ethical aspect to what I wrote—especially if I learned to write well. To be careless with power is the height (the depth) of arrogance.

Honor the world by observing it truly and writing about it with humility.

And, though I remember the piece almost word for word, I destroyed it. My name should never be attached to such self-congratulatory freedoms. "Look, ma! No hands!"

Let me quote Wendell Berry's essay "The Responsibility of the Poet" (1988). It explains the "badness" of that story which I could not keep. Wendell writes:

> *A poem reminds us also of the spiritual elation that we call "inspiration" or "gift." Or perhaps we ought to say that it should do so, it should be humble enough to do so, because we know that no permanently valuable poem is made by the merely intentional manipulation of its scrutable components. Hence, it reminds us of love. It is amateur work, lover's work. What we now call "professionalism" is anathema to it.*

Next Berry distinguishes between what he calls "professional" standards and the standard of love:

> *Professional standards, the standards of ambi-*
> *tion and selfishness, are always sliding downward*
> *toward expense, ostentation, and mediocrity. They*
> *tend always to narrow the ground of judgment.*
> *But amateur standards, the standards of love, are*
> *always straining upward toward the humble and*
> *the best. The context of love is the world*

By these definitions, I hope no longer to write stories, novels, plays in order to manipulate worldy minds,
works that titillate worldly ears and earn the applause
of worldly cash. Instead, I strive to write whatever is
true, whatever is honorable, whatever is just, whatever is commendable. If there is any excellence, and
if there is anything worthy of praise, I now think on
these things.

8. Ethical Obligations: 2

A N OFFICER OF THE LAW is a functional citizen of her community. Whether she deals with one felon or five children or five hundred demonstrators, she imposes her will, legal or illegal, upon them.

So too is the artist a functional citizen. But (1) because his work can't help but reflect his context and his community, and (2) because that work goes far beyond that community itself, and (3) because his attitude regarding his artistic profession affects the way he affects his community, it is necessary that he consider what will, honorable or dishonorable, prophetic or merely censorious, he shall impose upon the members of that community.

Certain artists deify their muse so that it becomes the all-consuming mandate of their lives. Their talent, they believe, the transcendent experience of sacred inspiration and its product, must at all costs dominate. Everything else takes second place. His family is expected to obey the artist's artistic ventures. It commands them, but not lovingly. Such loveless commands become taskmasters without reward. Forced to obey impossible commandments, commandments at which they must surely fail without the hope of forgiveness.

And because everything might be material for his art, the artist can feel justified in sacrificing anything upon the altar of his exalted profession. Or else he will disregard the cut-and-slashing of his pen upon good people.

Years ago a movie producer asked Horton Foote to write a screenplay based upon several stories in my book *Miz Lil and the Chronicles of Grace.*

Foote had won two Academy Awards, one for his script *To Kill a Mockingbird* and one for *Tender Mercies.* There was no question about the skill and the value of his art. There could have been none better than this playwright to translate anyone's stories by his craft.

Each of my stories had been based on my family. This time, however, I had learned not to place them in a bad light as I had by fiction in the eighth grade. The tales were true and honorable.

Horton and I met for two weeks in New Harmony, Indiana, so that he could research the background of my storied experiences. I was, as you might imagine, delighted to be in the presence of a man I so much admired, and gave myself over to his inquisitions.

But I had already edited things in order to make them both artistic and presentable. The harder experiences had no place in public.

Nevertheless, Horton probed and probed. He wanted to get behind my choices.

Now, Horton Foote was a southerner, a most gracious man. He spoke in a soft voice, ever courteous, almost reverential. It was his habit to sit—though I might stand and pace—and write his notes on a yellow legal pad.

When I demurred over some detail, he'd ask me to spend the night recollecting what I said I had forgotten. When I came back in the morning, repeating that my memory remained hazy, he quietly said, "No. You remember that."

The man was insistent.

Finally I began to make up a backstory. He had no right—however splendid his work—to break into what I determined must remain private.

I take nothing away from the body of the work he has bequeathed to posterity. Horton Foote is one of those artists who has joined the great and lasting tradition of English literature. But at the time it was my foolish, juvenile thought that he was not considering the effect his work would have upon his subject. "Foolish," I say, because he was so much the better artist.

Saul Bellow would also transfer his people (his wives) from real experiences to his novels, and do it so obviously that anyone who knew him knew the behaviors and the transgressions of those around him. His fiction is clearly autobiographical.

As for me and for the sake of the communion in which I live as a busy citizen not unlike the cop on the corner, I keep covenant with my family, my people, my town, my commonwealth. I honor what they in good faith have allowed me to see.

Nor do I believe that this restricts the full truth of the substance of my writing. Instead, I take these narrows as a challenge the same way a poet obeys the narrows of the strict form of a sonnet. It requires creativity to turn the contradictions between my community and my art into a story whole.

Surely, one can use an actual experience as the *model* for such experiences among all humanity. Witness Tennessee Williams in *The Glass Menagerie*. William Faulkner's use of the characters he knew in Oxford, Mississippi. James Joyce's *Dubliners*. Shakespeare's sonnets.

This method works better than merely changing names and places, therefore assuming that events have been well hidden. "Hidden" or not, they remain obvious to the people who people them.

Alternatively, the writer may choose to write on behalf of the community. African griots remember and tell the histories of their tribes past and present. The plains Indians did in past ages keep what they called a *Waniyetu Iyawapi*—a "winter count"—of the tribal events of the past year which they painted as pictographs on tanned buffalo hide. I have written some of my stories as chronicles of the inner city congregation under my pastoral care. In all these instances the stories are preservations of a people. They cannot be inventions. They cannot merely glorify, though they may elevate certain individuals while excoriating certain others. I have considered myself as a chronicler for the people of the inner city neighborhood where Thanne and I lived and worked for fifteen years.

At the same time, I cannot objectify the people of my community. That is, I can't divorce my own accountable self from them in order to study them, scrutinize, criticize, examine, analyze them as if they were a smear on a slide under a microscope. I am *of* my community. I owe them my moral consideration.

I know a woman in a small Michigan town who lives in a large house with a wrap-around porch and gingerbread dormers. To the glad fascination of her neighbors, a movie crew selected her house to be one of the sites in a full-length feature. Well, the woman agreed, of course. Technicians, cameras, equipment, cables, and lights cluttered the street and all her yard around. Actors acted. The director directed.

She invited members of her family to come from far distances to enjoy the heady experience with her.

The crew took measurements of the interior of her house. They shot pictures of the rooms. They developed their own blueprints, though they told her they didn't intend to disrupt her life by actually taking over and enacting scenes inside the house itself. Rather, they would build a duplicate on the movie set.

Then they left.

"Eighteen months," they said. "The movie will be released in eighteen months. It'll be an action film. We'll do one of the premiers right here in town."

So the woman waited a year and a half, cooling her anticipations.

When the premier took place, several hundred people came to watch it.

And when the premier was over, the woman was humiliated.

Her beloved house had become a nest of evil. Its perfect interior was used to symbolize a creeping insanity. Its very walls seemed to stink with sin.

The film was a hit.

Thereafter even tourists came to see her looming horror. Strange people pointed. Children shivered.

The house that had been in her family for three generations had been ruined.

For the sake of a well-paying product, careless of the people abused by its making—and therefore unethically—a producer had wounded one good woman.

Ovid boasts:

Est, Deus in nobis; agitante calescimus illo:
Sedibus aethereis spiritus ille venit.

"There is a god in us," he writes of writers. "We grow hot at his urging: that spirit comes from thrones ethereal."

But those who are seized by that god may feel as if they've suffered a theft. Something significant in their identities has been stolen and handled, *hand*-dled, *man*-handled. And the artist shall have assumed ownership of the community's precious thing.

A shared ownership (consider Homer, Beowulf, the Pentateuch, the tales of indigenous people—all of which are of the people and *for* the people) need not be baneful. The theft is to pluck something good from the ground that nourished it, and to use it without devotion, but rather as food for a bottomless god.

II. Practical Advice

9. Lunch Bucket Labor

WRITING IS A JOB LIKE any other. A factory worker, an office clerk, a doctor, a garbage collector all have to be at work by a certain time. And their work is done in a certain place. So it is with a writer.

Establish the place where you will do your work—always and always do your work. I know of certain authors who could work anywhere—Rainer Rilke, Henry James—but most of us don't store everything in our minds as if they were suitcases. On the other hand, place itself can store not only the progress of our work but our minds also.

Promise yourself to stay at your desk for a certain number of hours, beginning at one designated time, ending always at another. Then obey both time and place day after day and week after week. Don't wait for some burning inspiration to rush you into fresh material with excitement and delight. The flame of inspiration soon gutters out, and then where will you be? When inspiration comes (when, a friend of mine, a composer, says, "When the moose—the muse—kisses me on the nose.") it's best to be at your desk, working hard. And yes. Work hard. Be busy.

Like the laborer, rise from bed. Eat breakfast. Brush your teeth. Dress for work, then go to your room—better yet, go to your word-room in some other building—and sit and start to work.

Returning to such a workplace, you won't have to gather together your necessary books. They will be there, already waiting for you.

The books I choose to have at hand are a large dictionary and whatever volumes I need for research. These I keep on shelves close to me. As I continue on a particular project, I build a library of those books which are related to my topic. A thesaurus is okay—but only after you have become familiar with the various meanings of a thousand words in order to select the best alternative. Otherwise the shadings of a certain word will sound and seem to your reader completely out of place. A self-important word stuck into a common sentence will cause the reader to stop and wonder at it. You never want the reader to pay attention to a word itself. The words must vanish so that the reader can *experience* the narrative.

This is one reason why I refuse to allow a designer of my children's picture books to give colors or strange shapes to individual words. This may cause the words themselves, and not their purposeful effects, to catch at a reader's eyes and snatch their imaginations from the world the story builds.

For most of my writing life, I've used a typewriter. This way I was simply recording on paper sentences already composed in my mind, and I didn't have to break the flow of *my* imagination. Thought followed thought in an intimate succession. But when I began to work on the computer, when I could delete and change things in an effort to improve what I had written, I found myself interrupting that mental flow. I became too conscious of small mistakes, and I had to find that flow over and over again. Such interruptions seemed to me to have become make-work then. So I had to pretend that the computer was a typewriter after all.

As far as the break that a day and a night imposed on my writing: I learned to dovetail yesterday with today. I recommend the following solution:

At the end of every workday, print out what you have written. Next morning reread yesterday's work, pencil-editing the pages as you go. *Then* begin on fresh material. You will have returned to yesterday's flow, and the writing will slide easily from the old pages into the new.

I am a fiddler. I mean that when I'm stuck on an image or the construction of a thought, I will get up and pace and fiddle with something else—maybe vacuuming the carpet or making a cup of coffee—all the while allowing my unconscious brain to work the problem out. Once it has, immediately I sit and keep on writing.

Generally, I don't give two hoots for something called the "writer's block." It often results from a profound dissatisfaction with what has already been written, and therefore from an inability to heap bad stuff on worse stuff.

But you can always write *something*, even if it's terrible. Don't throw up your hands. Don't let dissatisfaction sink into despair.

I have to admit that some very important writers, like Lionel Trilling, suffered genuine periods of writer's block because of severe inner torment. He was a Jew seeking tenure, and this was a period, the mid-1930s, when Ivy League colleges—specifically Columbia University—invoked quotas to restrict the number of Jewish professors on their faculties. Members of Columbia's English department felt that Trilling, a "Freudian, a Marxist, and a Jew" as they called him, lacked the proper credentials, which is to say, he was not a white Anglo-Saxon Protestant.

Nevertheless, in 1641 Ben Jonson wrote:

> *If his wit will not arrive suddenly at the dignity*
> *of the Ancients, let him not yet fall out with it,*
> *quarrel, or be over hastily angry. Cast not away*
> *the quills yet. Nor scratch the wainscot. Beat not*

the poor desk—but bring to the forge and file again.

Turn to the new.

So what if you fall into a patch of bad writing. Write anyway. At some point, good will emerge from the bad, and you can continue working with a greater confidence.

Moreover, if you want to save some part of the bad, think of revision as forgiveness. Go ahead and make a mess of it, but truck on. At your first pass, sin boldly and fearlessly against the standards of your craft and your own expectations. Then, once you've gotten your stride back, return, revise, and grace will cover you.

10. The Literary Tradition

R EAD. READ. READ.
          Never cease to read what has been well
written in the past. Make your own what Ben Jonson
calls "the dignity of the ancients."

This, I suggest, is how you may "make it your
own": dwell in the literature. Live in it as if it were your
house. Better than analyzing it (which places you *outside* an artist's work, using your intellect only), allow
your imagination its full range and thereby *experience*
it.

After that you may go back to the beginning and
self-consciously parse for yourself its form, language,
metaphors, texture—everything of value that it has to
teach you.

Already in elementary school (as I have mentioned) I
knew I wanted to become an author. In graduate school,
then, I didn't enroll in creative writing classes. Rather, I
earned my master's degree in English literature. It seemed

to me that it was better to ground my creativity on solid traditions rather than on the business of creativity itself.

Learn well your great ancestors and the present practitioners of good craft, or else your work may not find place within their long histories.

T. S. Eliot writes in his essay, "Tradition and Individual Talent":

> *No poet, no artist of any art, has his complete meaning alone. His significance, his appreciation is the appreciation of his relation to the dead poets and artists. You cannot value him alone; you must set him, for contrast and comparison, among the dead.*
>
> *I mean this as a principle of aesthetic, not merely historical, criticism.*

What the critic looks for, the individual writer must perform. But when he performs it, he affects the whole body of literature.

> *What happens when a new work of art is created is something that happens simultaneously to all the works of art which preceded it. The existing monuments form an ideal order in themselves, which is modified by the introduction of the new (the really new) work of art among them. The existing order is complete before the new work arrives; for*

the order to persist after the supervention of nov-
elty, the whole existing order must be, if ever so
slightly, altered; and so the relations, proportions,
values of each work of art toward the whole are
readjusted. And the poet who is aware of this will
be aware of great difficulties and responsibilities.

What a wonderful thing, to shift the whole of Shake-speare's work and Chaucer's and Whitman's and the short stories of Eudora Welty all by your own addition!

Therefore, read, read, read.

What they have done will shape what you will do without your having to strain at it. Your very language will become enriched. You will not have to restrict it to one voice only, but will have a panoply of possibilities, all without effort.

BUT BE CLEAR ABOUT the sort of writing you want to do.

A good mystery novel is very good, even if it doesn't pretend to be literature. So write mysteries according to that genre's form. But learn the form first—by reading mysteries.

Entertain your readers with comedy. Observe how the best comedians do it. People are refreshed by enter-tainment.

Write for television. It is a most respectable profes-sion. Well-paying, too.

Study the classic movies. View them over and over
until you've conned the craft of the director, and the
camera of the D. P. (director of photography), and the
cuts of a good editor. Read the film scripts themselves.
Sit in theaters. Enjoy films both popular and independent. Then write screenplays. Even if your scripts
are not made into movies, producers may pay a pretty
penny to own them.

Fantasy. Science fiction. Picture books.

Novels for young adults can be literature. There is
surely a hungry market for them now.

Some of my students write articles for newspapers
and magazines.

One of them makes a very good living by writing
speeches (and jokes) for politicians with lumbering
tongues and for corporate leaders with no imagination
at all.

Be a *good* and well-read preacher.

Write letters more beautiful than most. John Keats
did. So did Heloise in the twelfth century. Abraham
Lincoln. Flannery O'Connor.

John Donne wrote devotions of superior intelli-
gence and faith. He wrote prayers.

The Celts wrote prayers.

Origen incised heretics with a devastating pen.

Martin Luther wrote hymns.

But how will you know these things, and how will

you climb their ladders to excellence, if you do not read?

Read!

You will have already noticed that I keep naming authors and their works. I will continue to do so. This is to introduce you to the tradition you'll want to know and to read—a vast company of your ancestors and colleagues, those who precede you and surround you now. I offer a partial library for your own improvement.

Whether you maintain a journal or not, your memory is like a shadow-room with a thousand shelves. On those shelves rest materials from your past experiences (lived experiences together with experiences of the imagination which other authors have granted you). While you write, when you come upon a blank spot, these experiences and their details will present themselves. You'll take down the one that best suits your need. It is all available to you. You will have *two* libraries, then.

Here are two examples from *The Book of the Dun Cow*:

The novel narrates three battles between the community of "good" animals and the offspring of "evil." In the second battle, Chauntecleer the Rooster (our hero) fights against Cockatrice (a legendary figure that is part rooster and part serpent). At the end of that battle, Cockatrice falls upon Chauntecleer who is lying on his back. Cockatrice is stabbed by one of Chauntecleer's spurs. So intent is Cockatrice upon killing Chauntecleer, that he drives the spur farther into his body in order to reach our hero's throat. It is a ghastly act: evil will sacrifice its own life to take the life of its enemy.

This scene did not spring from my own imagination. I took it down from my mental shelf.

At the end of Sir Thomas Malory's tale of King Arthur and his knights (written in the fifteenth century), Arthur must fight his own son, Mordred. Arthur pierces Mordred with his spear. But Mordred's hatred of his father is supernal. He thrusts the spear through and through himself, until he is close enough to dispatch Arthur with his own sword. They both die.

As with Mordred, so with Cockatrice.

My second example:

Before the three battles take place, Chauntecleer and his wife come upon their three chicks—their children—who lie dead. While they approach the children, still ignorant of the tragedy before them, we watch their coming through the eyes of another character, Russel the Fox, who knows what Chauntecleer and Pertelote are about to find. The Fox is already suffering, grief-stricken and agonizing over the encounter soon to come. But he stands separate and can do nothing but watch and await the tragic discovery.

Again, this particular device wasn't first mine. I took it from one of the Icelandic sagas that Snorri Sturluson (early thirteenth century) preserved. Two armies are marching to war. Neither one knows how close the other is, for they are approaching each other on opposite sides of a high hill. On top of that hill a shepherd can see both armies coming. The shepherd is, therefore, the only one who knows of the bloody war about to take place. The reader too knows. So the reader shares the shepherd's point of view. The suspense tears the heart of the shepherd and the reader both. Since that ancient scene had affected me, I hoped to affect *my* readers the same.

These two examples are meant to reveal the rich trove you have at hand, and to persuade you of the importance, of the *necessity*, of reading. Reading.

11. Keep Your Day Job

JOHN GARDNER URGES WRITERS TO get paying jobs. Almost all writers are poorly paid, and poets worst of all.

But Gardner has another reason for his recommendation. Whatever we do, it will draw us out of our tendencies to be reclusive. It will place us in conversation with folks, which conversation cannot help but enrich our experience (with, say, students, mill workers, criminals, customers, courtroom judges, and lawyers). Too, whatever job we hold will expand our brains and feed our imaginations.

William Carlos Williams was a physician. T. S. Eliot was an editor. Wendell Berry is a farmer. Wallace Stevens was the vice president of an insurance firm in Hartford, Connecticut. George Herbert, a pastor in England, Gerard Manley Hopkins a Catholic priest, and so forth.

Gardner himself was an academic, a Ph.D. professor, a philosopher, and a medievalist.

It's not hard to see how these pursuits shaped his literature.

Read his novel *Grendel*. Gardner's protagonist—Grendel—is a refashioning of the monster that lurked violently outside of Hrothgar's meadhall, ever ready to eat his warriors. The long poem *Beowulf* is an epic written sometime in the eighth century, during the Middle Ages. In Gardner's hands the monster is to be pitied for his rage and his despair. His rants are existential, and therefore wholly modern. But the novel would not have been written if Gardner had not been so familiar with the stuff of his paying job.

More than that, the novel offers one of the best explanations I've ever read about the power of language actually to create what had not been before. A blind singer comes to Hrothgar when his warriors are completely demoralized. The singer sings of their past so powerfully that they get off their butts and build a new, most marvelous meadhall—a building that had existed only in the singer's mind until it existed as wood beams and shelter on a very fine hill.

By song the singer created, Gardner declares, almost as God had created the world by speech.

His day job shaped his writing, for he wrote in the forms and according to the techniques of the ancient philosophical writers: Socratic dialogue, allegory, dialectic, fabulism.

For years and years my paying day job was the

pastoral ministry. I served a small, inner-city African-American congregation. How else would I have learned and lived and loved in a culture not my own? How else would I come to receive the affection and the trust of these people, and only thereby begin to understand racism from the inside, the gestures, the language, the little cuts of oppression, the difficulties of the poor—all of which have found place in my books? I discovered the power of storytelling among those who lived by story.

And I walked the neighborhood; was propositioned by prostitutes; suffered with the sick; laughed at a raucous, street-wise humor; visited young men in prisons; prayed over the dying; became intimate with people in their most private affairs; married them, baptized them, catechized them, and agonized through their divorces; received a dear affection that elevated myself—and was granted a wealth of human insight I could never have earned, except that I kept my day job.

I raised chickens, and chickens populated my first novel.

There are certain authors, yes, who closed themselves off from the world, such as Marcel Proust who wrote the long, complex *Remembrance of Things Past*. But he was endowed with a natural run of liquid language and a frightfully precise memory. All he needed he had already lived. You may be Proust, but it's unlikely. Assume that you are not.

12. Observe Accurately

WHAT PEOPLE GENERALLY RECKON AS the "real" world—everything visible and experiential around them—my author-eye must observe with a dead-eyed accuracy in order to get it (the description, the setting, the ways things actually happen) right.

Does the wind *really* moan? Well, no—not unless there is some obstruction to give it voice, like telephone wires or tree boughs or the soft sifting of dry snow. When a child lies on her back in bed and weeps, how can her tears "stream down her cheeks"?

No description should come from a writer's false presumptions of how the universe works. A writer cannot live entirely within himself and expect to present the true world to his readers. The canny reader will lose trust when he cannot accept such silly mistakes. And once trust is lost in small things, it will be lost for the story whole.

So then: a character cannot suddenly change in

order to accommodate the plot. If a writer wants a certain thing to happen, he can't force it. It must derive from the natural *development* of that character. This is the organic motion of the first covenant.

I myself broke that covenant in my novel *The Crying for a Vision* by giving a two-foot depth of snow a crust hard enough to support the weight of a walking boy. Such a crust is possible, of course. But not, as I wrote thoughtlessly, on the same cold day in which the snow first fell. *That* snow would be soft. It needs several days of sun and wind to harden the surface, a wet freeze, a sunlight thaw, and a freeze again.

If I had caught my error before the book went into print, I would not have grumbled for running up against a stupid choice. I could have arisen to the challenge of the contradiction between my plot and its setting. In order to do right by both, I should have been forced to take certain creative leaps which would move the book in directions so new and unpremeditated that I myself might be astonished.

In fact, it is right here, in these leaps, that creativity is most wonderfully challenged.

The German philosopher Hegel developed a system which I use to explain this spurt of creativity. On the one hand, I know where the plot must go: this is the "thesis." On the other hand, my covenant declares that I cannot go that way: this is the "antithesis." But I must honor both, which seems at first an impossible dilemma. Then, suddenly, I find the means to marry them together. This is the leap. It is the synthesis, and the synthesis is compacted by creativity.

So then—back to perceived reality. How *do* houses creak? And why? And when?

And how is sadness expressed in a face? (It is simply not enough to say that a child is "sad." A reader cannot experience what a reader cannot see.) Consider the puckering of a child's chin and the tug of her lip. And what does sadness feel like?

With this last series of questions we move from the realm of the natural world into the behaviors of human beings, our multitudinous interactions, our gestures, facial expressions, moods, developments, loves and hates and fears and delights, the subtle relationship between our interior selves and their exterior manifestations. We move into the realm of social experience. Here especially (as this is nearly always the central stuff of a story, its force and its purpose) I must observe with a dead-eyed accuracy.

And how shall I best observe the human behavior around me?

Without prejudice. With *humility*.

If I see what I already expect to see, I will see nothing new.

Or, to put it another way: if I think I know what I do not know, I will never know it.

Observe with a self-acknowledged ignorance.

To shed all the prejudgments by which we live and make decisions is a frightful prospect. We must become strangers in a strange land.

My mother's method for teaching me how to drive a car was to put me behind the wheel and command me to drive—on the busy Harlem Avenue in Chicago and in the night and in the rain. It scared the be-dickens out of me. The car was a VW bus with a long, trembling stick shift and the windshield mere inches before my face. I could not make sense of the lights all up and down the avenue: shop-window lights, streetlights, headlights, the light skimming off the wet pavement before me.

And then my mother started to scream, "Christmas tree! Christmas tree!"

Dazzled and confused, I would make no decisions at all. So I hit the brakes and stopped in the middle of the street.

"Finally!" my mother said.

"Christmas tree?" I asked.

And she said, "Didn't you see all those taillights ahead lighting up like a Christmas tree?"

Then, I drove in ignorance, frightfully. Nowadays, I know which lights direct my driving and am oblivious to all the rest. I drive, as it were, according to certain prejudgments. I come with expectations already in place.

But the writer must observe as if driving on Harlem at night and after a rain. Danger makes for sharp and watchful eyes. It tunes my ears and makes my very flesh alert. After a while, though, it isn't danger that persuades me to pay attention. It is the willing confession of ignorance and a patient watchfulness.

To be humble is to make a nothing of myself. Every human being before the writer is a mystery. He ought not to put people into his own procrustean bed, forcing upon an infinite population only a handful of "characters" he already knows and expects to find.

In order to "get it right," watch *for* the truth, not *with* the truth, as if it were a donkey's tail to pin on the persons you write about.

Again, how shall I best observe the human behavior around me?

With a *sympathetic* imagination.

"Sym-pathy" derives from two Greek words: *syn*, which can be translated "with." And *pathos*, which denotes feelings, emotions, sufferings, experiences. It is not enough merely to observe the details of others' lives. I must also *participate* in those lives, as if I took up my dwelling inside of them. The locus of my point of view cannot start from my own dispassionate, external eye, but rather must start in their hearts in order to see through *their* eyes.

In order to protect herself, an abused child or

woman learns to interpret the face of her abuser, the timbre of his voice, and the chop of his gestures, in order to know his mood even before he does. This is a form of sympathetic imagination, seeing from the inside. It is possible that such troubled childhoods have trained so many artists to create persons not themselves, and to do so with persuasive power, causing the reader likewise to experience that character's peculiar personality and his many emotions.

Though George Eliot (Mary Ann Evans) was not a man, she wrote with a trenchant authenticity from within the minds of men.

William Styron was not black. Neither did he live during the years of American slavery. Yet, in *The Confessions of Nat Turner*, he produced a rebellious slave genuinely African American, intelligent, angry, charismatic, and ultimately defeated. Styron was assailed for thinking a white author could represent a black man accurately. But that came from a politics of cultural separation and not from the genuine experience of art.

Nobody blames Shakespeare for his overweening presumption that he could understand people not of his own gender. Keats said of him that he had "negative capability." It enabled him to "get right" the forceful Lady Macbeth, gentle Ophelia, old anguished and delusional Lear, the soldiering Othello. The writer negates his self in order to write from within the souls of other selves.

While I was doing research for *The Crying for a Vision*—a novel about the Lakota Indians a century ago—I was invited to attend a Sun Dance on the Rosebud Reservation in South Dakota.

I realized that the novel could not be authentic if I had only read about their ways, no matter how many books I gathered, no matter how well I could teach myself the language from books. So I went. It was my plan to take notes of all I saw and heard. That, surely, would "get it right."

But when I turned my van off a county road and onto a rutted dirt path to the place of the dance itself, I was stopped by two large-chested Indians. There was a closed gate ahead of me. I could see brilliant white tipis in the distances, leaning toward the sun. The men wanted to interrogate me.

"Do you have a camera?" they asked.

I answered, "No."

"Do you have a tape recorder?"

"No."

"Do you paint? Are you going to paint pictures?"

Well, "No."

With that they let me pass.

They had not asked me whether I was going to take notes.

It was then I realized the fault of this part of my research.

The Lakota did not want objective watchers at

their sacred ceremony. Such people could not but be separated, and such separation would make for a foreign presence. They sought a spiritual participation. I decided not to take notes, but rather to put myself wholly into their hands—as much as possible to be in the Sun Dance and not at it, for that is the deepest level of authenticity.

Over and over again between rounds of dancing, the old man who held the microphone said, "You are our brothers. Here in the sacred circle [the *cangleshka wakan*], you have become my brother."

But of the anthropologists who attended, the Lakota said, "They are anthroes." It was meant as a gentle joke. The two anthropologists at that Sun Dance performed all the maneuvers of the dancers. Nevertheless, they were not kin. They lacked the one thing necessary: to believe in God as the Lakota did, as the Lakota knew that I did.

13. Some Notes Regarding the Long-Distance Novel

WHEN WRITING FICTION IT HELPS to set a sign ever before your eyes which reads: "What's happening?"

Watch your story unfold as if it is a movie which you are recording in your own words.

Your question is not "What does this mean?" but "What are the characters doing now? What are they saying? What's the weather? What time of day? Where is the action taking place? What, whether inside a character or around her, is *happening*?"

This reduces an author's tendency to talk *about* things rather than allowing the action itself, a character's gestures, her expressions, her dialogue, to present the readers plain details with which they can themselves interpret, just as they do in real life.

You want them to *experience* the events by your objective art, and not to get bogged down in an intellectual essay or in the effusion you write for your own sole pleasure.

In this manner you honor your readers' personal capacities. Telling them too much demeans them, as if they are children who need loads of explanations.

IF I HAVE THE barest sense of my novel's general direction, I will write anything that might begin to reveal more than I know. At this point I'm utterly free, because these beginnings are for myself alone.

My father once told me that after he finished an important letter he deleted the first paragraph since it consisted of his personal preparation to write the necessary stuff.

Likewise, your first chapter or so can find the voice and the tone that will prevail, or the overarching intent of the novel, or various characters with which to people it. Whatever you write, however it gets you into the true narrative, you can edit out your early wanderings.

Next, when I've collected a cast of interesting characters and have discovered the general sense of my novel's direction, I begin with something I call the "slingshot." That is, I give the characters a brief problem and then watch to see how they will solve it. The problem need be no more than something cartoonish. And the characters are still flat. But their action (as I follow it rather than produce it) will define them and their relationships to one another. Things like that. How do they act? How do they interact? What comes naturally, and what have I forced? What setting works? Indeed, what setting was necessary to elaborate their problem? What must now issue from this brief "slingshotting" into the narrative whole? By the time the characters come up with a solution, I have learned (earned) the answers to my questions.

But each one must become a full figure independent of my self-conscious creating. For me this occurs when one of them suddenly says something altogether right, but which takes me by surprise.

From that point on I can as much listen to that character as control what he speaks.

As I continue to write, then, I will talk with the character, as it were, asking whether we ought to go in this direction or else in that one. Which leads to a dead end? Which opens new doors ahead of us? I will imagine the best sequence of events, then sit and write them down.

Writing a long novel is like throwing stones ahead of me into a rushing stream of water. I step on the near stone, then throw out another, then step on that, then throw out another—for the novel is written like babies born of a marriage. I am one partner, the novel as it has been written to this point is the other partner, and what is to come is the issue of our continuing dialogue. Writing is discovering.

I cannot contradict what has already been written! This rule narrows the possibilities and sharpens the narrative's future. The further I go, the more I know about the plan of the plot, and the fewer are my choices. It now is the characters' personalities and the tightening reins of the action that work toward an ending—and now a pure, intense creativity is called for in order to weave of the few elements left to me a right and satisfying conclusion.

I often think that the approach to a conclusion is like docking an ocean-going vessel. Both require a hundred adjustments long before the dock—the ending—is reached.

But when a proper, compelling conclusion eludes me, when I can't imagine the one that honors the whole rest of the novel, then I search the body of my manuscript where I might find the seeds of an ending after all.

William Stafford in *Writing the Australian Crawl* counsels young poets, when they are stuck, not only to spend time rereading what has been already written, but even to repeat a good line and go from there.

One of my students, Jason by name, wrote a short story about a boy (himself) fishing with an older man in a rowboat. The boy is only now learning the harsh indifference of the world. This is obvious from the progression of the tale. But the ending was tacked on and neglected altogether the story's theme.

"Go back. Read what is already written. Something might make a right conclusion after all."

The student did. He found a small memory the older man tells the boy. There is impact in the memory, worthy of drawing out into a full event. And since endings are as important—if not more important—than beginnings, he transferred the old man's brief memory to the end.

The memory: when *he* was younger, the man baited his hook with a small frog. Then when he cast it out, and the line unreeled with a zinging sound, a bird flew down and snatched the frog away, snapping the line.

This is as good as Tennyson's description of nature, "red in tooth and claw."

Like Jason, it may be that a subtler, closer reading of your manuscript can lead you to a better sense of an ending.

Watch whether certain of your images develop through the book, though you had not recognized this while you created them. Robert Bly offers the example of containers: a jar grows into a house, the house into a home, and the home into the concept of a structure that holds things together. In the end it is "safety" that emerges—a reaching for, a motion toward safety. Your unconscious shall have led you to the deeper theme and its more complete conclusion.

"By indirections find directions out."

REGARDING THE VOICES OF my characters:

Even when a comedian tells a tale before an audience, she varies the ways her characters speak. That way she need not persistently name this one or that one in dialogue. Neither does she have to use "he said" or "she said." The patter can go faster and faster. And the action begins to zip by.

Just so do I at the beginning of the novel consciously give each character a different set of tones, speeds, vocabulary, the qualities and patterns of their sentences.

In his short story, "A Clean, Well-Lighted Place," Hemingway presents long, uninterrupted patches of dialogue between two waiters in a café. In fact, the whole story is almost only dialogue.

> *"He's drunk now," he said.*
> *"He's drunk every night."*
> *"What did he want to kill himself for?"*
> *"How should I know."*
> *"How did he do it?"*
> *"He hung himself with a rope."*
> *"Who cut him down?"*
> *"His niece."*
> *"Why did they do it?"*
> *"Fear for his soul."*
> *"How much money has he got?"*
> *"He's got plenty."*

"He must be eighty years old."
"Anyway I should say he was eighty."
"I wish he would go home. I never get to bed
  before three o'clock...."

And so forth.

If you try to distinguish the two waiters from the beginning to the end, you'll find that Hemingway himself loses the distinction between them, so that by the end of their conversation one waiter has been exchanged for the other. I wonder whether this may have happened because the author uses his own plain, abrupt voice for both waiters throughout the story.

Popular fiction can get away with using one voice for all its characters. It's the plot that's most important. But literature has to do better.

Listen to Blanche and Stanley in Tennessee Williams' *A Streetcar Named Desire* (even their names show that they come from different cultures and classes of people):

Blanche: Hello, Stanley! Here I am, all freshly
  bathed and scented, and feeling like a brand
  new human being.

Stanley: That's good.

B: Excuse me while I slip on my pretty new dress.

S: Go right ahead, Blanche.

*B: I understand there's to be a little card party to
    which we ladies are cordially not invited.*

S: Yeah?

B: Where's Stella?

S. Out on the porch.

B: I'm going to ask a favor of you in a moment.

S: What could that be, I wonder.

B: Some buttons in the back. You may enter.

S: You look all right.

B: Many thanks. Now the buttons.

S: I can do nothing with them.

*B: You men with your big clumsy fingers. May I
    have a drag on your cig?*

It is immediately apparent that Stanley speaks in
short barks, while Blanche uses long sentences. His

talk lacks all imagery and adjectives. Hers uses cultured (if worn) coquetry, an excess of cute "little," "pretty" adjectives, and a highborn sense of herself.

Not only does their language distinguish the woman from the man, it also reveals their separate backgrounds, their education, their personalities. And as the play moves toward its climax, their talk intensifies without losing the distinction.

Shakespeare in *King Lear*, when Lear and a Fool are in foul weather on a heath:

> *Lear: Blow winds and crack your cheeks! Rage,*
> > *blow,*
> > *You cataracts and hurricanes, spout*
> > *Till you have drenched our steeples, drowned*
> > > *the cocks.*
> > *You sulphurous and thought-executing fires,*
> > *Vaunt-couriers of oak-cleaving thunderbolts,*
> > *Singe my white head! [...]*

> *Fool: O, nuncle, court holy-water in a dry house is*
> > *better than this rain-water out o' door. Good*
> > *nuncle, in, ask thy daughters' blessing: here's*
> > *a night pities neither wise man nor fools.*

> *L: Rumble thy bellyful! Spit fire! Spout rain [...]*
> > *I tax not you, you elements, with unkindness*
> > *[...]*

F: He that has a house to put 's head in has a good
   head-piece [...]
There was never yet fair woman but she made
   mouths in a glass.

I leave it to you to hear how a lightsome fool and an explosive king use language which distinguishes not only their characters but also their moods.

Once, somewhere near the beginning of a novel, I have identified the various speeches of my people, I will write out some telling phrase for each and keep the phrases close at hand. Then if I lose the sound of a voice as the novel continues, I'll return to my written phrase in order to remind myself of its voice-tones, languages, vocabulary, etc., and keep on writing.

Listen to the dialect in which Uncle Remus (Joel Chandler Harris's "The Wonderful Tar-Baby") tells his stories:

One day ater Brer Rabbit fool 'im wid dat cal-
amus root, Brer Fox went ter wuk en got 'im some
tar, en mix it wid some turken time, en fix up a
contrapshun wat he call a Tar-Baby, en he tuck
dish yer Tar-Baby en he sot 'er in de big road....

Actually, I think Harris took the dialect too far. He might have spattered Uncle Remus's speech with fewer bits of dialect and have gotten the same effect without causing his reader to stop, to become too conscious of the words themselves by trying to sound them out. I myself stalled on "bimeby." I sounded it at first as "by-mi-bee" till I finally realized that the word meant "by and by."

So much for the sounds. What about a person's visual description?

It isn't enough to describe a character only once when she enters the narrative, and then leave it up to the reader to continue "seeing" her as things progress. The reader must *keep* seeing the subject. Therefore, choose a particular characteristic and refer to it often, but variously, whenever she appears. For example, do her fingers flutter at her hair? Does he continually look askance, unable to keep his eyes fixed on someone else? What about clothing? Shoes? Dapper or sloppy? Does a woman dress in baubles? Does a man smoke a pipe? Does he always carry a bumbershoot? What does he *do* with his bumbershoot?

The more my characters develop, the more I enjoy the pleasure of their company. It's a fine motivation to stay my course through the many seasons it takes to finish the long-distance novel.

PACE THE NOVEL BY moving back and forth between humorous situations (if there can be humor) and serious ones. Each will intensify the other. And one will relieve the reader a while, like the buzz of liquor before returning to a hard sobriety.

Ken Kesey in *Sometimes A Great Notion* actually collides humor and tragedy together. One character is given to a boisterous, infectious laughter. Readers laugh along with him. He *is* a funny fellow. But then he is caught wedged in a river as the water rises. When it reaches flood stage, it covers his face. The protagonist can see his friend under the water. He tries to save him by sending an air hose down to his mouth. But the funny fellow finds humor in the situation and begins to laugh. It is his laughter that loses the hose and sucks water and drowns him. And for us, it is the laughter that makes this scene so dreadful.

Move between long sections of prose and easier sequences of dialogue. When a reader turns the page and sees short paragraphs of dialogue, she will anticipate a quicker, more pleasant experience.

Likewise, let brief chapters interrupt extended ones. In his novel *As I Lay Dying*, William Faulkner never imposes his own authorial voice on the narrative. Each chapter is the monologue of one character and another, and Faulkner names each for its speaker. No two voices sound alike.

Some monologues continue for many pages. Others consist of single paragraphs. And one is only one line long. Vardaman says: "My mother is a fish." That's the whole of it.

Though the novel runs to 250 pages, it *feels* short.

And when the action of *your* novel speeds up, keep to a restless shortness. Tighten your sentences to a rat-a-tat rhythm.

Choose one particular point of view and stick with it.

The omniscient POV can be aware of everything and anything that occurs in a narrative. But it must never seem to trick the reader by leaving out information simply to have it jump out later: "Surprise!" This is manipulation. A reader will cease to trust the author who plays with her mind. And mistrust will destroy her willing suspension of disbelief, which will destroy her ability to experience the art, which has fallen into ineptitude.

If you choose a third-person POV, I suggest that the reader should always know *which* person's sight and insight is active at any time. And then you must not offer some detail that that person could not know—whether consciously or unconsciously. For example: if a character is, let's say, inside an airplane, you will break his POV by suddenly describing the *outside* of the plane as red. You can allow something to occur out of his sight if by some other means he can sense it. The airplane's landing gear goes down. That's okay, if the wheels cause a *whoosh* when they catch the open air.

Once again, read *As I Lay Dying*. Absolutely nothing happens except it is within the speaker's purview.

On the other hand, Faulkner implies for his reader so much of which his character is ignorant. It is a fine display of craft. And the craft is something you can learn.

Help yourself by locating your creating self not in your own mind, nor in the fingers at the keyboard, but in the character whose POV is active. Dwell in that character. *Become* that character. Then you will not have to break your brain to get it right. "Right" will come naturally.

The first-person POV, wherein there is but one narrator, puts even greater strictures on the novelist. Now *everything* the reader knows must come through the speaker's telling, through her imagery, her emotions, her particular personality, the breadth of her sensory capabilities, and the depth of her interpretation.

In Hemingway's *A Farewell to Arms* the narrator is the major character in the novel, one Frederic Henry. So closely does Hemingway hone to his narrator's POV that the man's full name doesn't appear until the thirteenth chapter when someone else speaks it. Why would he say it, unless it is forced into the narrative in order to accommodate the reader and not the story? Otherwise, other characters refer to him by his rank: "Tenente," "Lootenant."

Joseph Conrad uses this device in his novel *The Heart of Darkness*. The story is related almost completely through the eyes of a seaman named Marlow. In this case the narrator is a minor character. This POV and this novelistic form restricts the author almost as much as a sonnet does a poet—but what a delight to accomplish the more difficult thing!

So is F. Scott Fitzgerald's narrator in *The Great Gatsby* a minor, twenty-nine-year-old character named Nick Carraway. Carraway remains ignorant of the facts of Jay Gatsby's life, ignorant of his motives and his deeper personality, until the end. In fact, it is the mystery that creates the greater suspension.

Gatsby's past life is stitched throughout the novel by Fitzgerald's crafty use of a literary technique called "retrospective narration." Previous events propel the story to its conclusion—but Carraway cannot account for the gap of five years (1912 to 1917) between the last of Gatsby's past and their first meeting. *This* is the stuff we don't know, and its revelation makes up the power of the conclusion when Gatsby, floating on an air mattress in his swimming pool, is shot dead.

One further restriction on the author's craft is to create an unreliable narrator. This figure does not always tell the truth. She may know the truth but distort it for motives of her own. She may *not* know the truth, and so the distortion occurs on account of her natural character. Perhaps she's too young to realize what she's saying (as is Scout in *To Kill A Mockingbird*). Perhaps she's shut up in a cell.

The device is called "dramatic irony." There is an evident contrast between what the narrator knows (even about his own actions) and what the reader can divine. Now the reader is invited to engage in more than simple experience. She can enter into an interpretive dialogue with the novel. This novel *needs* its reader. The reader is its balance and its ballast—and a savvy reader is glad for this greater participation.

DURING THE COURSE OF my first novels, I experienced a weird separation from the real world. My work became my reality. I dwelt in it even when I wasn't actually writing. And when something popped me out of my imaginary world it was not like waking from a dream, but like sleeping *into* a dream.

The real world seemed all out of its proper proportion. Somewhat false, strange, illusory. I forgot common courtesies and daily duties. I lost the *me* in me.

Friends began to worry.

They asked my wife whether I was suffering some disease. Depression, maybe? Or: why was I angry all the time?

Not angry, of course, but oblivious of their kindly conversation.

In the end I needn't have worried. All this resolved itself into the pedestrian business of writing and writing, and weirdness retreated into a dull, persistent company.

WHAT DO YOU THINK of those for whom you write? What is your attitude toward your reader?

Contempt? Scorn? They will show.

A cold reproval? It will inform your tone.

A prophetic scolding? But will your reader believe you have the authority to scold like Moses standing on the mountain?

A joint laughter at the folly of society? Join Joseph Heller in *Catch-22*. Learn of him.

A common sorrow for things unfulfilled, or delight in things sweetly fulfilled? You will your readers into your confidence and form a community of familiars.

Affection? Read Kurt Vonnegut.

Love? Love is service. Love contracts relationships of honor and elevation. Love is not envious or boastful or arrogant or rude. It doesn't insist on its own way, is not irritable or resentful, does not rejoice in wrong-doing, but rejoices in the truth.

FINALLY, I BELIEVE THAT there are (as least) four virtues for the long-distance writer:

1. A good *memory*.

Not only will the author not contradict what has already been written, but a present solution might be discovered in something written in the past.

The cartoon/slingshot with which I began *The Book of the Dun Cow* involved the menace of a Rat—Ebenezer Rat—who ate the Hens' eggs before the chick-child was born-hatched. There seemed nothing good in this slickery fellow with his long, licorice tail. Chauntecleer, Lord of his Coop, dispatched Ebenezer and denied him entrance into the Coop forevermore.

At that point I thought I was done with the Rat.

But much later in the novel I needed to communicate to Chauntecleer that an ineluctable evil was stealing into this land. Ebenezer Rat, who had left the narrative, had not left my memory—and suddenly he became the evidence of evil drawing near. He is found dying from bites of the wicked Basilisks. And his own character is enriched by his return, for the dying raises sympathy for him who had been merely bad.

Often a creative leap is accomplished by rooting through the body of a work.

Moreover, a good memory can save a novel from progressing in a merely linear fashion. There is little strength in the book that moves from episode to episode, each episode relating only to the one before it. The plot dips down like a long cane pole, becoming ever weaker as it goes. A reader can lose trust in the author and interest in his novel.

But a persistent cross-referencing of images and characters and events produces a novel that builds its house geometrically. *This* is how the world works. Nothing happens in isolation. A birthday party, for example, remembers parties past, recollects characters we haven't seen in a while, ages the characters one year more so that the reader feels the effects of time, and also experiences the development of the *whole* plot in a single day. Now we have not a nodding pole, but a tough, universal structure.

2. *Patience.*

Sometimes a writer will rush ahead of himself, borne along by the story in his head before he writes the story down where his readers can find it. He's unaware that he is, in fact, merely sketching scenes, heaping new stuff on stuff he only imagines he's laid down before. But if this is the case, he cripples his going and clothes his scarecrow in tatters. He switches styles and tones to serve the galloping plot. He falls into clichés. He mixes his images rather than allowing them to grow in kinship with one another. (Shakespeare clustered his images, returning to them again and again, but always as themes with variations. Note the imagery of rot which runs through every act of *Hamlet*.)

Patience will work through every detail of a scene, and these well-composed details will become the solid provenance of scenes to come. They will also send you on routes a sketchy outline could never even contemplate.

So then: sweetly question the scene before you. Does the dialogue sound like the natural talk you hear around you daily? Does the dialogue (different dialects in different mouths) reveal character as much as it offers information? And does it give more than information? Does it both inform and further the plot? What *minor* gesture (you'll get the grand ones easily enough) unlocks a whole trove of meaning? What sort of light falls upon the scene? Have you forgotten the passages of day and night, evening and morning? And which are the sticks with which you will construct the scene that comes next?

3. *Risk.*

That is, don't be too nervous to write yourself into the darkness of unknowing.

Poets do this all the time.

Do I contradict suggestions I've made above? Yes. It requires the author to write according to two distinctly different minds. But the one (clarity about the narrative already written down, by which its future is illuminated) can feed the other (sudden bursts of probabilities as yet unforeseen).

The wonder is that the novel might plumb depths beyond your own God-given personhood. It might, therefore, change a good novel into the sort of literature a good critic can interpret, showing *you* meanings you did not know it had.

The fear, on the other hand, is that you might so misdirect your novel that you might never find it again. Hence the risk.

But nothing is ever lost. If your wild flight crashes, go back to the material in which you are confident. Reread it slowly to find the person (your person) who wrote it, and tune your voice to that voice again.

But nothing is lost. What you wrote in darkness cannot help but inform and enrich what now you write in the light.

Even before I began to write *The Book of the Dun Cow*, I had its title. During my graduate study in medieval literature I came upon an incunabulum which had been bound in cow's leather. Over the centuries the leather faded, becoming a drab *dun* color. It tickled me to think of a book that gave the lie to the old platitude, "You can't tell a book by its cover." Here was a book which was named *for* its cover.

I never doubted the appropriateness of my title, though I wrote nearly half the book without a dun cow anywhere in it. I was writing into the darkness. But in order to make the title right—always watching for the opportunity to make it right—I was able to introduce my Dun Cow at a time when the main characters were despairing. And behold: because she entered their despair, what else could she be but consolation itself? The title demanded a Dun Cow. Her placement shaped her character, and she became more than I had it in me to create.

Now and again, risk rewards the intrepid writer.

4. *Trust.*

I can't believe that the genuine author writes for himself or herself alone. They write in order to be read. Art is an event in two parts. The artist acts. The artist produces a work which in itself has the potential (but only the potential) to become art. It is when the reader acts—picks up the book and reads it—that art is fully present and presently fulfilled.

And what sort of reader does the self-conscious writer seek? Well, someone who is at least as smart as he is, maybe smarter.

When T. S. Eliot published his long poem "The Waste Land" as a book, he added notes which explained its more obscure elements. If his reason for doing so was, as it has been said, to bulk out what otherwise would be too slim a volume, making it look more *like* a book, then I have no objections. But if he wrote the notes in order to explain things to ill-informed readers, then I do object.

Trust your readers. There is no need to make accommodation for them—not just in notes but also in explaining your literary allusions, simplifying matters you think too complex for them, *telling* them what they should think about this and that. Such accommodations reveal that you hold them in a low opinion, and a good reader is liable to be offended.

But your trust will encourage you to ascend new heights of literature, carrying the readers along. In consequence, *they* will trust your writing, and they will be happy to spend money on your next novel. Trust begets trust. Your audience will grow book by book. Reviewers and critics will take interest in your work. Then, whether or not you bring in a haul of loot, you will have arrived.

14. Revision

I HAVE ALREADY SPOKEN ABOUT the pencil editing of yesterday's work.

Now I suggest that a single revision of the whole work is not enough. Expect to be at it three, four, or many more times. Between one of these versions and the next it will be helpful to allow months to pass so that when you return to the text, you'll do so with a fresh mind. The time between will allow your unconscious mind to pick through the manuscript, hitting on new ideas, developing characters that had otherwise been insignificant, and, perhaps, imagining a new subplot.

Ask other people wise in the craft to read and to comment on your draft. Their eyes can improve the piece in ways you would never have considered. Before he published his remarkable poem *The Waste Land*, T. S. Eliot gave the manuscript to the poet Ezra Pound. He asked Pound to judge the poem's many fragments, which had incorporated a variety of voices and characters. Would Pound likewise assess the poem's literary value, its historical allusions, the bits and pieces of contemporary life, its reading of the historical past, its use of myths and legends? Pound returned the poem to Eliot with great slashings. Eliot agreed.

After cooling your work and yourself, read the whole piece as though you were yourself a new reader. You'll be able to notice certain big sections which can either be deleted or else moved to another place in the manuscript. It's possible that what you've written in one spot has already been handled in another.

Gustave Flaubert spent five years on *Madame Bovary*. It's not unusual for an author to devote as many as ten years to a novel of important literature— not necessarily because she is stuck, but rather because she is striving for the best and cleanest book according to her own standards.

Watch for smaller mistakes.

Again, Flaubert: early in *Bovary* he describes Madame Bovary's eyes as having one color. Later in the same novel he forgot that first color and gave her eyes another color altogether.

All his life long Walt Whitman never ceased to revise his book of poems called *Leaves of Grass*.

I never revise by snippets. Nor do I use the computer to switch chunks from one place to another. It's

my contention that certain words and sentence con-
structions, imagery and metaphors and tones and style
are often used even when I'm unaware of them. They
follow in a natural and seamless whole.

But if, later, I begin to revise individual passages, I
may be in another mood or may have become a different
person, living under other circumstances. Consequently
I will bring to these passages—again, unconsciously—a
different set of moods, metaphors, etc. And my reader
will sense these passages as foreign interruptions.

Therefore I keep my entire previously-printed manuscript at my elbow and start the revision from scratch.
This way, however different is my present personhood,
the difference will affect the whole, not a part.

Patience, friend. Don't do as I have done. I've been
too quick, rushing a new draft straight to the publisher
when it was undone and messy. It used to be that editors were willing to do the work of true editing.

An example of such an editor is Max Perkins at
Scribners, who worked in the first half of the last century.
When Thomas Wolfe submitted a sprawling manuscript
of something like one thousand typed pages, Perkins
exhausted himself by reorganizing it and cutting it by a
third. It appeared under the title *Look Homeward, Angel*.
Wolfe's second novel, *Of Time and the River*, required a
full eighteen months of revision.

Wolfe wrote longhand, throwing the finished pages
on the floor behind him.

One night Thomas Wolfe strode through New York—a tall, lanky-legged young man—repeating in a loud voice, "Wrote ten thousand words today. Wrote ten thousand words today!" This picture gives us an insight into why the manuscripts he gave to Perkins were so monstrous and unready.

My own first editor, Joanne Ryder at Harper & Row, helped me enormously with *The Book of the Dun Cow*. And I am fortunate in having an editor who will still offer suggestions: Bob Hudson. But he is unusual.

Nowadays editors have become acquisition editors only, looking for new authors or authors with previous publications and a loyal audience. They want to receive the submissions already perfected before they will accept them for publication.

I SUPPOSE YOU ALREADY know not to love your "babies" too much. Your own critical eye should persuade you to cut parts you think are striking or good simply because you created them. What to you is a beautiful born infant, to somebody else might seem to have a squashed face, eyelids as puffy as a soaked bean seed, a mottled red complexion, and a pointy head.

What will you do, then, when somebody says, "Delete your baby"?

Before I submitted *The Book of the Dun Cow* to Joanne Ryder, I had sent her an earlier novel of mine.

She wrote me a kindly letter which said, "This is unpublishable." Then she went on to reveal two errors which threaded all the way through my manuscript and therefore crashed the novel completely. This had become a grown-up baby. Nevertheless, I scrapped the book. Joanne had persuaded me, and I was willing to be persuaded.

But this editor-stranger had written me a letter!

I wrote her back asking whether I might send her my next manuscript. Would she be willing to look at that one too?

She said, "Yes."

Within a year, I finished *Dun Cow* and mailed it off. It took six months before she answered.

When she did, she said, "We can't offer to publish it yet."

Not *yet*. Maybe later?

That's when I, on my own recognizance, accomplished a full revision, but didn't send it. Perhaps I could find another publishing house.

Then, late in spring there suddenly came a new letter with the news that the book was accepted.

I wrote immediately, "Tell me what I have to do," and in a cocky allusion to David Copperfield, wrote, "Barkis is willing."

Barkis had a hungry appetite and was fearless. All that summer I revised. I chewed on and swallowed her every suggestion. ("You don't need that first chapter.

Cut it.") In autumn 1976 she liked what I had done, and the book went into production. Its first edition was released in 1978. *The New York Times* selected it as the best children's book of the year. For this first book I received a National Book Award. Simon and Schuster bid against other houses and won the right to bring it out in paperback. It was translated into ten other languages. It was published in Australia and South Africa.

None of which would have happened if Barkis had not been willing to revise.

I had no idea of the importance of the National Book Award. Therefore I didn't consider it all that necessary to show up in New York for the celebration and final announcement of the winners. William F. Buckley was the master of ceremonies. He was kind enough to send me my check ($2000) and a profound sculpture by Louise Nevelson. Nor did I fully understand the importance of that old lady, the *Times*. I thought that this was what happened to writers generally.

I experienced my most fulfilling award on an Amtrak train bound for the west. One evening my young son Matthew tugged at my sleeve and pointed to a man across the aisle. He said, "Go tell him who you are." For the man was reading a paperback *Dun Cow*—and was chuckling to himself over the funnier bits in it.

I did not embarrass myself by interrupting his cheer with my pride.

ANOTHER SORT OF REVISION altogether can elevate
your work from one level to a higher one. What may
already have been published can be reshaped and published again in a new venue.

I wrote a short piece for the members of my congregation in the church newsletter. By accident I learned
that the piece was being used in homiletic classes in
my seminary in St. Louis. Well, if it was good enough
for theologians, it should be good enough for a wider
public. Therefore I reused the article in a column I was
writing for a Scripps Howard newspaper. I entitled it
"The Ragman."

Soon I learned that camp counselors and other
religious leaders were telling the story without naming
me as the author. So I took "Ragman" to the next level
by making it the first chapter in a new book. This way
the article would be clearly under my own copyright.
Anyone who thought to tell my story again should
have to ask me first.

But no one did ask me. They used it as they had
before, and it spread throughout the country by word
of mouth.

Perhaps a year later a film producer called,
requesting the right to turn "Ragman" into a movie.
I began to negotiate a contract that would benefit me
as much as it did the producer. Finally, he stopped the

proceedings. He said to me, "My lawyer says I don't need your permission at all. Your story has been so widely disseminated without the author's ascription that it's in the public domain."

It began to appear on the web. People were telling the tale as if they themselves had created it. When my secretary emailed these people, informing them that they should have requested my permission first, some deleted it from their sites, others humbly asked what they must do to make it right. But several wrote me scathing letters, saying that what we do we do for Jesus, and why should they pay to serve the Lord? Didn't *I* want to serve the Lord in the same spirit as they did?

But artists need to be paid to live and support their families. When churches use the songs of composers without permission or compensation, this is a kind of theft.

So my advice is doubled: elevate your material as you have the chance.

But copyright it in order to keep it your own. And always note with the copyright that it cannot be used without the author's permission. This for the work you publish.

As for material yet unpublished, don't fear that some unscrupulous publisher or producer will steal your stuff or plagiarize it. Since you will have kept copies of your revisions and of the final draft, US laws declare those alone as proof of your copyright, whether you signal it on your manuscript or not. Nor do you have to establish copyright in Washington. Your written evidence is quite enough.

15. Preparing to Publish

I F YOU ARE STILL IN college or graduate school, in English or in creative writing or in some sort of communications, look around you. One of your classmates may become an editor of books or magazines. Establish relationships. Talk literature. Keep contacts far beyond graduation, and you will already have met the one who can help you in the future.

Attend as many published writers' readings as possible, then talk personally with the writer. Ask if he or she would be willing to exchange letters.

Make a list of all the living authors whom you admire. Send them letters (not emails, since emails seem too evanescent and deletable). Send them letters out of the blue. When you do, write knowledgeably about one of their pieces, showing a genuine ability to interpret the piece and do so with (not overblown) admiration. Or see if you can't publish an article regarding their word (if nowhere else than in a school newspaper or journal). Then send that to them, always with the suggestion that you may share letters thereafter. After the first letter, once someone has answered you, *then* send one or two of your strongest (but shorter) works. It's more likely that a busy writer will read it and respond.

Don't contact just one or two, but as many as you can.

Maybe most will never answer. Nevertheless, it's surprising how many authors take seriously an obligation to help the writers coming up behind them.

In these several ways I have made friends with such folk as Wendell Berry, Madeleine L'Engle, Larry Woiwode, the playwrights Mark St. Germain and Theresa Rebeck, the television writer and producer Jim Leonard, the poets Denise Levertov, Robert Siegel, Luci Shaw, Paul Mariani, Susanna Childress. Toni Morrison and Maya Angelou have endorsed my works.

What a wonderful company to be in!

Wherever you live you can find other writers of like minds. I think it's important to make promises to one another: regularly to meet, when and where; how best to critique one another's material. If you live at distances away from each other, use email. Or else move to a city where the authors gather (expatriates in Paris, writers in New York). It is best to meet face to face, because talk grows out of talk; and arguments are flint and steel; and discussion leads to deeper understandings, even to new literary movements; and ideas may leap immediately to mind which would be lost in the slower method of letters. Discuss old, admired art, new and developing art, and the judgments of national critics.

Coleridge had his Wordsworth. Walt Whitman his Emerson. Shakespeare his Ben Jonson. Addison his Steele. Heloise her Abelard. The Rossettis one another. Plath her Hughes. You know of the Inklings (C. S. Lewis, Tolkien, Charles Williams), the Bloomsbury Group, the Harlem Renaissance, the Black Mountain Writers, the Beats.

As for yourself, find ways and venues for giving readings of your own work—in the schools where you are and in groups with which you have relationships.

BEFORE YOU SUBMIT WHOLE books, gain a reputation by publishing smaller pieces in journals and magazine. This requires a heavy commitment to plain business which is not the writing itself. Enter your work in publishers' contests. There are many awards for unpublished authors. Attend writers' conferences where you may make friends and find helpful critics; but assess which conferences are serious and best for you, since many are used by poetasters as an annual gathering with acquaintances, something like a vacation.

Once it was possible to send a submission "over the transom"—that is, to send your manuscript cold to a publishing house in the hope that an editor might pick it from the slush pile and read it. Now most publishers read manuscripts only if they come not from the author but from the author's agent. And editors have become acquisition editors, whose job is to seek new, unpublished authors and to work with manuscripts already ready to print.

If you still want to send your material directly to a publisher, then seek out smaller companies. Perhaps your manuscript fits their narrow guidelines: feminist literature, geographically limited books (such as the Northwest or the particular state in which you live), science fiction, historical fiction, African American, Latin American, sports stories, mystery, dark humor, and so forth.

And once upon a time, those authors who paid to self-publish their books were beneath attention. But now a new route to self-publishing is considered honorable. Sell it digitally, direct to the reader. The writer's percentage of sales is much higher than if she had to divide the purchase price with a book publisher.

The drawback here is that one must promote and advertise one's own material. Lacking contacts with reviewers or the money to buy space in various publications, you might schedule your own readings and ask newspapers to send reporters. Ask friends to email friends who would email *their* friends, and so forth. You might yourself hire a savvy marketer. It is not altogether impossible to make friends with a patron who admires your work and would be willing to support you in your efforts.

Potential agents are listed in such books as *The Writer's Market*. Check online for the description each offers regarding his and her business. Agents will often name the people in their "stable" of authors. If among their authors you find one or two who write the same sort of material you do, approach that agent. Approach *many* such agents.

I have used the following method.

After choosing agents who lived in a single city where agents most gather (New York or Chicago or L.A.), I wrote them letters (not emails) informing them that I would soon send them, in a different envelope, my most recent manuscript together with a brief biography and a list of anything I'd published: articles, short stories, poems, columns. In the same letter I said that after a month or so I would telephone them in order to set up an appointment. Again, agents often indicate online the length of time they take before responding to queries. I referred to that timeline in order to schedule my calls according to their own working patterns.

Then I did call them, one by one, asking to meet face to face. Some said, "Don't bother." But others were quite willing to meet me.

In order to make the best use of my time, I set the appointments all in a single week. Then I traveled to that city, keeping as many as three appointments a day.

We discussed the sort of writing I did, both in the present manuscript and in the future. I took notes. Perhaps there were questions I could answer better later. In no case did I at that meeting expect or want an answer. Instead, I asked them when they would be ready to respond, and then told them that I would telephone again.

For most of those agents, that was our final communication. They explained that they didn't think we were suited for each other. This wasn't rejection, nor was there anything to be upset about. It was business.

But one man was enthusiastic. He became the agent to whom I am still attached.

16. Save the Old Stuff

THROW NOTHING YOU'VE WRITTEN AWAY. And rather than storing your work in your computer only, print the pages, save them on paper, and file the paper in some kind of labeled order.

There are a number of reasons for this suggestion.

First: even though your first use of certain material appeared in a failed manuscript, there will have been valuable stuff in it, and you will find place for it in later works. These may be an image, or a well-written paragraph, or a fine description, or a nascent idea just a-borning, or a character, or an event. If it is filed, you can find it quickly and lay it open on your desk and reuse it.

Second: you don't yet know whether you will become an important writer. If you do, someone is sure to research your work. He or she will want to know *how* you worked, what you revised and in what sequence. How can your critics or your biographers probe these things if you haven't saved them?

For example, we have several versions of William Blake's poem "The Tyger." The changes he made in this poem contain the development of his thought and of the growth of his poetic sense. We would not know Blake so well without such evidence before us.

Third: make archives of your material. One day you may want to bequeath these archives to some university's library. Perhaps a graduate student will need them for a dissertation. He will thank you to find so much in one place.

For the same reason, save copies of all your letters—even of the quick notes you've sent to publishers, friends, relatives, and colleagues. What you email might otherwise be lost.

My stuff is boxed and even now is being stored in Valparaiso University's library. This is where I've taught for twenty years. I don't myself have to arrange it. In time Valpo will do that labor. They also get my lecture notes and copies of the speeches I've made over the years.

Moreover, I have put restrictions on their use hereafter, and the library will obey my wishes. There are personal letters I don't want made public until a certain number of years after my death. These include, for example, letters I sent to my wife before we were married in 1968, letters to my children during hard times and good, letters I sent home when I was nineteen years old and hitchhiking through Europe. Desperate letters, angry letters. Herein is my private life.

Do you see how early in your years you should start saving things? Saving *everything*?

On the other hand, I once poured out rants in a ledger book. These were not general rants. They were about acquaintances and my own kin, and should be destroyed, never to be seen at all.

THERE YOU HAVE IT, my good and studious young writer—advice from an old-coot writer. Take what seems good. Ignore what seems lesser, as you will. Reread it all, underlining and making notes in the margins.

Prepare.

Read good literature.

Rub your chin and think.

Write a paragraph.

Don't delete it.

Write a page.

Write on until the work has discovered what it wants to be, and you have begun to find your voice.

When and if the first draft needs more attention, keep it, work with it, but start the next draft at the beginning.

All will be well. And all manner of thing very well.

Walter Wangerin, Jr.
July 13, 2016

Also by Walter Wangerin, Jr.
(from Rabbit Room Press)

EVERLASTING IS THE PAST
A Memoir

Play: *RACHEL WEEPING FOR HER CHILDREN*
(Epiphany)

Play: *THE WAY OF THE CROSS*
(Palm Sunday)

Also available from
RABBIT ROOM PRESS

THE WISHES OF THE FISH KING
by Douglas Kaine McKelvey
Illustrated by Jamin Still

FAR SIDE OF THE SEA
by Eric Peters

THE MOLEHILL
A literary menagerie

THE WINGFEATHER SAGA
by Andrew Peterson

THE WILDERKING TRILOGY
by Jonathan Rogers

and more at store.RabbitRoom.com

The
RABBIT ROOM

The Rabbit Room is a 501(c)(3) not-for-profit orga-
nization. We foster Christ-centered community and
spiritual formation through story, music, and art.

For more information about the Rabbit Room and
Rabbit Room Press, visit about.RabbitRoom.com.

Coming in 2017 from
RABBIT ROOM PRESS

HENRY AND THE CHALK DRAGON
by Jennifer Trafton
Illustrated by Benjamin Schipper

RABBIT ROOM
— P R E S S —